NEW MERMAIDS

General Editors:
William C. Carroll, Boston University
Brian Gibbons, University of Münster
Tiffany Stern, University of Oxford

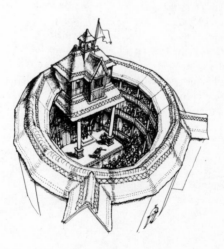

Reconstruction of an Elizabethan Theatre
by C. Walter Hodges

NEW MERMAIDS

NEW MERMAIDS

CHRISTOPHER MARLOWE

EDWARD II

Edited by Martin Wiggins

Fellow of the Shakespeare Institute
University of Birmingham

Text edited by Robert Lindsey

Revised with a new introduction
by Stephen Guy-Bray

University of British Columbia

Bloomsbury Methuen Drama
An imprint of Bloomsbury Publishing Plc

B L O O M S B U R Y
LONDON · OXFORD · NEW YORK · NEW DELHI · SYDNEY

Bloomsbury Methuen Drama

An imprint of Bloomsbury Publishing Plc

Imprint previously known as Methuen Drama

50 Bedford Square	1385 Broadway
London	New York
WC1B 3DP	NY 10018
UK	USA

www.bloomsbury.com

BLOOMSBURY, METHUEN DRAMA and the Diana logo are trademarks of Bloomsbury Publishing Plc

First New Mermaid edition 1967
Copyright © 1967 Ernest Benn Limited
Second Edition 1997
Reprinted with new cover design 2003, 2005, 2006, 2009, 2015 (twice), 2016 (twice)

Revised edition with new introduction © 2014 Bloomsbury Publishing Plc

British Library Cataloguing-in-Publication Data
A catalogue record for this book is available from the British Library.

ISBN: PB: 978-1-4725-2052-4
ePDF: 978-1-4725-7540-1
ePUB: 978-1-4725-7539-5

Library of Congress Cataloging-in-Publication Data
A catalog record for this book is available from the Library of Congress.

Series: New Mermaids

Typeset by Country Setting, Kingsdown, Kent CT14 8ES
Printed and bound in India

CONTENTS

ACKNOWLEDGEMENTS

The Introduction to this revised edition is the work of Stephen Guy-Bray; the text and commentary were prepared for the original edition by Robert Lindsey and Martin Wiggins in collaboration.

I am grateful to Tiffany Stern for asking me to write the introduction to this new edition of *Edward II*. It has been a very interesting and rewarding project. At Bloomsbury, I thank Margaret Bartley, Claire Cooper, Simon Trussler, and Margaret Berrill for all their help and hard work. My colleague Vin Nardizzi read the first draft of the introduction and made many helpful comments, many of which I actually followed. And I thank Julie Beebe for giving me such a wonderful place to write.

STEPHEN GUY-BRAY

Our paramount debt is to the General Editor, Brian Gibbons, whose painstaking and exacting work has significantly improved the edition, especially in matters on which we ultimately had to agree to differ. In the early stages of preparing the edition, Dr L.G. Black gave valuable advice and guidance, Simon Markham made useful suggestions on the text and notes, and Roma Gill gave both encouragement and the benefit of her knowledge and experience. In the later stages, we have further benefited from the textual expertise of John Jowett and the wisdom of Stanley Wells. We have been fortunate in dealing with librarians and archivists who fully understand the needs of the researcher, particularly Susan Brock of the Shakespeare Institute library, Stratford-upon-Avon; James Shaw of the Shakespeare Centre Library, Stratford-upon-Avon; Susan Knowles of the BBC Written Archives Centre, Caversham; and Richard Bell of the Bodleian Library, Oxford. Among postgraduate students, Rebekah Owens shared the results of her research on Kyd's letter to Puckering, and Solitaire Townsend, Shaalu Malhotra, and Sue Taylor all helped to locate material relating to the stage history. Paul Edmondson, Jeremy Ehrlich, Eugene Giddens, Mary McGuigan, and especially Jane Kingsley-Smith made an invaluable contribution to the proof-checking. At A. & C. Black, Anne Watts has been a supportive and sympathetic editor, and we could not have hoped for a better job of copy-editing than we received from Margaret Berrill. Others who have helped in various ways, great and small, are Kelley Costigan, Lorna Flint, Andrew Pixley, Trefor Stockwell, Keith Topping, and The Malone Society.

MARTIN WIGGINS AND ROBERT LINDSEY

INTRODUCTION

About the Play

Christopher Marlowe has been a highly regarded and highly controversial writer since he first became famous in the mid-1580s as the author of *Tamburlaine*. While *Doctor Faustus* is probably still his most famous play, *Edward II* has become increasingly popular and increasingly widely studied in the last few decades. This is for a number of reasons. For one, as a history play *Edward II* provides a usefully different approach to the question of the representation of English history from that of Shakespeare's plays. While Shakespeare's history plays, broadly speaking, rely on an attitude toward kingship that is never really interrogated, Marlowe's play – his sole history play – calls into question the nature of English kingship itself. In this respect, *Edward II* makes an interesting pair with Shakespeare's *Richard II*, which also tells the story of a 'weak' king, although this comparison will show the extent to which Marlowe's critique of monarchy is more thorough than Shakespeare's.

Edward II has also been of tremendous importance in the field of sexuality studies, an area that has become one of the most important fields within Renaissance literary studies over the course of the last thirty years or so. It has long been recognized that much Renaissance literature interrogates traditional ideas about gender roles and about the forms of sexual expression deemed permissible or impermissible in the sixteenth and seventeenth centuries, but in many of the texts studied from this point of view – the comedies of Shakespeare and Lyly are an obvious example – the theme of sexual transgression is treated with some caution and the texts in question usually end with the reemergence of the traditional sexual order.

Plot Summary

Edward I banished Piers Gaveston, his son's lover, from England. As the play opens, Edward I has just died; the new king, Edward II, has called Gaveston back from France. While the two men are overjoyed at being reunited, their attachment is viewed with increasing disfavour by Edward's wife Isabella and by a powerful group of nobles, led by the Mortimers (younger and older) and the Earl of Lancaster. The nobles succeed in getting Gaveston banished but, on the advice of the queen, they recall him so as to have him under their control. After a series of skirmishes and pursuits, the nobles capture and execute Gaveston. Before long, Edward II finds a new lover (Spencer the younger) and civil war begins again. The queen and her lover the younger Mortimer defeat Edward and take him captive. Mortimer orders Edward killed and rules England through the queen. At the very end of the play, however, Edward's young son, now Edward III, takes control of his kingdom and orders the execution of Mortimer and the imprisonment of Isabella. The play ends with the tableau of Mortimer's head on Edward II's coffin.

The Author

Christopher Marlowe was born in Canterbury in early 1564, the son of a shoemaker who seems to have been both improvident and litigious. Marlowe obtained two scholarships that changed his life: the first, in 1578, was to the King's School in Canterbury; the second, a couple of years later, was to Corpus Christi College at Cambridge. This education enabled the young Marlowe to obtain the classical education on which so much of his writing depends and to rise above his family's social class. In *Edward II*, the scholar Baldock claims that 'my gentry / I fetched from Oxford, not from heraldry' (6.240–1); Marlowe could have made the same statement about Cambridge.

Marlowe began his studies at Cambridge in early 1581. He received his B.A. in February 1584 and his M.A. in 1587. This summary should not be taken to imply that his progress at Cambridge was smooth, however. For one thing, the expectation would have been that in going to study at Cambridge on the scholarship endowed by Archbishop Matthew Parker, Marlowe was destined to become an Anglican clergyman. While it is impossible to speak categorically about Marlowe's character, all can agree that he would have made a spectacularly unlikely vicar.

What is more, there were problems during his candidacy for the degree of Master of Arts. Although not all the details are known, it is clear that the University tried to prevent Marlowe from getting his M.A. on the grounds that he had spent too much time away from Cambridge. Nor, it appears, was this simply a case of failing to fulfil the residency requirements. There were rumours that Marlowe had gone over to Rheims, where there was a seminary that trained Roman Catholic missionaries to Protestant England. Marlowe was granted his M.A. as the result of the direct intervention of the Privy Council, which wrote to Cambridge to clear him of the imputation that he had sought to become a Catholic missionary. The Privy Council's letter went on, tantalizingly, to state that Marlowe 'had done Her Majesty good service'.[1]

The nature of this service is unclear, although both biographers and writers of historical fiction – two categories that are often difficult to distinguish in the case of Marlowe – have tended to assume that Marlowe was

1 *Acts of the Privy Council*, n.s. xv, 141.

a spy. Furthermore, the assumption has been that Marlowe remained a spy, and the narrative of Marlowe the secret agent has been extended from the Privy Council's intervention in his university affairs to include events in his later life, such as his arrest in Flushing (Vlissingen) in 1592 for counterfeiting and, especially, his violent death at the end of May 1593. While it is true that at that time Marlowe was under investigation by the Privy Council, there is no evidence that his death at the age of twenty-nine was anything other than one of the most tragic accidents ever to have befallen English literature. Indeed, given that Marlowe had twice been involved in violent attacks during his short adult life (in London in 1589, an incident in which a man was killed, and again towards the end of 1592 in Canterbury), being stabbed to death in a tavern was not, perhaps, an especially surprising end.

What is certain is that when barely twenty-nine years old, Marlowe had already achieved tremendous fame as a playwright – a success that his near contemporary William Shakespeare (only two months his junior) was still some years from equalling.

As is the case with much of his life, the chronology of Marlowe's works is not known for certain. It is generally assumed that his first work was *Dido, Queen of Carthage*. This play is usually dated to about 1586; the title page of the first edition gives as its authors Marlowe and Thomas Nashe, who had been at Cambridge at the same time as Marlowe, but it is not known what share Nashe had in the play. But the play that made Marlowe famous was *Tamburlaine*, the almost unbearably exciting story of the conqueror Timur Lenk, a story filled with violence, expressed in a singularly powerful and flexible blank verse, and – or so many of Marlowe's contemporaries thought – characterized by atheism. Indeed, *Tamburlaine* (and Marlowe's work more generally) has been of tremendous importance to the narrative of the emergence of the golden age of English theatre.[2]

Tamburlaine was probably first performed in 1587, and Marlowe soon followed it with a sequel (*The Second Part of Tamburlaine*). To this point, the chronology is fairly clear, but after these three plays came four more whose order is not known. The received order is *Doctor Faustus*, *The Jew of Malta*, *The Massacre at Paris*, and *Edward II*, which is usually dated to 1591 or 1592. Filling out this canon is his translation of Ovid's *Amores*, traditionally assigned to his years at Cambridge, and his narrative poem *Hero and Leander*, thought to have been written in the last months of his life when Marlowe was living in Kent after the theatres had been closed by plague.

2 In this connection, Patrick Ryan offers an important corrective that stresses Marlowe's continuity with medieval drama; see 'Marlowe's *Edward II* and the Medieval Passion Play'. *Comparative Drama* 32 (1998–9), 465–95. Ryan is especially good on Marlowe's handling of Edward's downfall and death.

Marlowe's contemporaries thought that his writings expressed atheism, or at least very irregular religious opinions. When Marlowe was under investigation by the Privy Council at the end of his short life, an associate of his called Richard Baines submitted a paper accusing Marlowe of both atheism and sodomy, memorably uniting the two in the claim that Marlowe had said that Jesus was the lover of St John.[3] According to Baines, Marlowe thought that the primary purpose of religion was to produce fear and thus to make people easier to govern. It has also been thought, then and ever since, that both his opinions on sexuality and his sexual practice were irregular. Homoeroticism plays a crucial role in *Edward II*; it is also significant in *Hero and Leander* and in *Dido, Queen of Carthage*. In other words, a significant portion of Marlowe's writings is concerned with homoeroticism; ever since, this fact has been taken to tell us something about Marlowe's own sexual practices.

The truth of the matter as regards Marlowe's private life will never be known. It is certainly not impossible that Baines, seeking to ingratiate himself with the Privy Council, wrote what he thought would please them. Still, while the evidence that Marlowe was an atheist and a sodomite is not conclusive, there is absolutely no evidence that he was orthodox either in his religion or in his sexual behaviour. This consideration has not, however, stopped generations of critics, anxious to preserve a great English author from what they would consider infamy. The concern of these critics for Marlowe's reputation would be merely quaint if it did not also have the effect of leading to homophobic analyses of his writings. This critical homophobia is especially noticeable (still) and especially harmful in the case of *Edward II*.[4]

Date, Source, and Productions

While *Edward II* is usually dated, as I have said, to nearly the end of Marlowe's life, there is no firm evidence for this. His primary source was the second edition of Raphael Holinshed's *Chronicles*, which appeared in 1587.[5] Marlowe also made use, to a much lesser extent, of chronicles by

---

3 For the Baines note, see Millar MacLure, ed., *Marlowe: the Critical Heritage, 1588–1896*, 1979.

4 For a practical discussion and summary of many of these homophobic analyses, see Stephen Guy-Bray, 'Homophobia and the Depoliticizing of *Edward II*', *English Studies in Canada* 17 (1991), 125–33, and Simon Shepherd, *Marlowe and the Politics of Elizabethan Theatre*, 1986, especially pp. 198–9.

5 For a good discussion of some of the differences between Holinshed and Marlowe, see Emily C. Bartels, *Spectacles of Strangeness: Imperialism, Alienation, and Marlowe*, 1993, pp. 147–56. For a good discussion of the importance of the chronicles to Marlowe's construction of the play, see Joan Park, 'History, Tragedy, and Truth in Christopher Marlowe's *Edward II*', *Studies in English Literature* 39 (1999), 275–90.

Robert Fabyan (1559), Richard Grafton (1569), and John Stow (1580). Thus, the play could arguably have been written as early as 1587, and as Henry III of France, a king popularly imagined to have been destroyed by his male favourites, was assassinated in that year an earlier date seems reasonable.[6]

On the other hand, we do know that *Edward II* was first performed by the Earl of Pembroke's Men, a company that was not recorded before 1592 (of course, that is not conclusive proof that it did not exist before that date). That the early 1590s saw a number of plays dealing with wars between English kings and their nobles, the most famous of which now is Shakespeare's *Henry VI* from 1591, could also be taken to suggest a date in the early 1590s. Both these facts make the later date plausible. The matter, like so much else about Marlowe's life and career, must be regarded as unsettled. No contemporary accounts of performances of the play survive; for this reason, not only the date but also the audience's reactions to the play and the manner in which it was performed are all unknown to us.

Edward II appears to have been performed as late as the 1620s, but then not again until 1903. Over the course of the last century, the play has been increasingly frequently performed, at first in England and then throughout the English-speaking world.[7] And beyond: Bertolt Brecht wrote a German version, *Leben Eduard Zweiten des Englands*, that has achieved some popularity both in German and in English translation, although it is not one of Brecht's best works.

Many celebrated actors have taken the title role. Particularly well-known among these are Ian McKellen in a 1969 production, which was broadcast the next year and which marked the first passionate male–male kiss on British television, and Simon Russell Beale in a controversial Royal Shakespeare Company production from 1991.[8] These and other productions in the last half-century could certainly not be accused of downplaying the homoeroticism of *Edward II*. Indeed, the theatrical productions of the play tend to be more radical than the critical analyses, at least in their presentation of the physical nature of male–male love.

---

6 A perceptive discussion of the play's relation to political debates about the role of favourites in the late sixteenth century can be found in Curtis Perry, 'The Politics of Access and Representations of the Sodomite King in Early Modern England', *Renaissance Quarterly* 54 (2000), 1054–83.

7 For very interesting discussions of the recent performance of the play, see David Fuller, 'Love or Politics: The Man or the King?' *Shakespeare Bulletin* 27.1 (2009), 81–115; Angela K. Ahlgren, 'Christopher Marlowe's "Unholy Fascination": Performing Queer *Edward II* in the 1990s', *Journal of Dramatic Theory and Criticism* 25.2 (2011), 5–22.

8 As of 2013, the production with McKellen was available on DVD through BBC video..

The most famous and controversial version to date is undeniably Derek Jarman's film version from 1991: *Queer Edward II*.[9] Jarman radically revised, shuffled, and reshaped Marlowe's play, setting it in a version of the conservative and homophobic United Kingdom in which he himself lived and died (in 1994). Jarman's greatest achievement was to emphasize the homoeroticism and the politics of the play, to demonstrate their crucial interconnection, and to insist on their relevance to his and our contemporary world.[10] It is no exaggeration to say that *Queer Edward II* achieved a similar, and similarly scandalous, success to *Tamburlaine*, usefully reminding audiences just how transgressive Marlowe can still be. While Jarman exaggerates the subversive potential of male homosexuality in order to make a point about twentieth-century homophobia, his film valuably brings together several of the play's themes and aspects that are usually considered in isolation. In effect, Jarman demonstrates that it is misleading to speak, as I have done here, of a private life, and this connection of the public (politics) and the private (sexuality) is indeed one of the distinguishing features of Marlowe's *Edward II*.

Sodomy

Edward II has typically been discussed as a play that is about homosexuality as much as (or more than) it is about anything else. But while critics writing in the first three-quarters or so of the twentieth century were content to use the words 'homosexual' and 'homosexuality', more recent critics have preferred to use a range of synonyms on the grounds that, following Foucault's influential *History of Sexuality* (1976; first English edition 1978), homosexuality cannot be said to have existed before the second half of the nineteenth-century. The word 'sodomy' is perhaps the most useful of these synonyms, as it has the merit of including Edward's love for Gaveston while not excluding many of the other relationships in the play.

The standard historical work on sodomy in the Renaissance is Alan Bray's *Homosexuality in Renaissance England* (1982). Much of what Bray writes has had to be qualified in the thirty years since the book was published, but it is still essential to the study of the topic (under whatever name). Perhaps Bray's most important point in the context of *Edward II* is that although sodomy was a capital offence for much of the period he discusses, prosecutions were very rare indeed. It appears that sodomy was

---

9   In 1992, the screenplay was published, lavishly illustrated with stills from the film.
10 Jarman's film has been the subject of many analyses; two of the best are Raymond Armstrong, 'More Jiggery than Pokery: Derek Jarman's *Edward II*', in *British Queer Cinema*, ed. Robin Griffiths, 2006, pp. 145–56, and Jim Ellis, *Derek Jarman's Angelic Conversations*, 2009, pp. 200–19.

only prosecuted when it was connected to a larger disturbance in the social order; much male–male sexuality was (tacitly) included under the heading of male friendship, which was considered the highest form of human relationship in Renaissance England.[11] Celebrations of male friendship are everywhere in the literature of the period, but as Stephen Orgel pointed out, 'the only dramatic instance of a homosexual relationship presented in the terms in which the culture formally conceived it – as antisocial, seditious, ultimately disastrous – is in Marlowe's *Edward II*'.[12] In this section of the introduction, I shall be concerned with the extent to which the sexual behaviour in the play is or is not connected to social disorder more generally.

The play's most explicit discussion of what we would now call homosexuality comes in the fourth scene. The elder Mortimer advises his nephew to make peace with Edward: 'Let him without controlment have his will. / The mightiest kings have had their minions' (4.391–2). Mortimer senior goes on to provide classical examples – Alexander, Hercules, Achilles, Cicero, and Socrates. In this speech, homoeroticism is clearly presented as no obstacle to the highest conceivable achievement in military or intellectual life: unlike sodomy, which interferes with the functioning of the social order, this homoeroticism can coexist with the status quo.

It is important to point out, however, that Mortimer's defence cannot be taken to indicate that the nobles tolerate other sexual practices instead, it means that they are willing to ignore their homophobia as long as the status quo is maintained. This is precisely the point that the younger Mortimer goes on to make in his reply. Beginning by saying that 'Uncle, his wanton humour grieves not me' (4.403), he goes on to complain that Gaveston is low born, that he spends money on pleasure that could be used to pay soldiers, that he wears very fancy clothes and jewels, and that he and Edward 'laugh at such as we, / And flout our train and jest at our attire' (4.418–19). Clearly, much of Mortimer's opposition to Gaveston is connected to what Amanda Bailey has perceptively described as 'the play's awareness of the potency of aesthetic defiance'.[13] Mortimer's stress on Gaveston's humble origins and the specific accusation that he is permitted to 'riot it with the treasure of the realm' (4.406) point to the connection with social disorder that turns the love between men from something that

---

11 These points are made throughout Bray's book; for a good brief treatment of the topic, see *Homosexuality in Renaissance England*, 1995 edn, pp. 70–2.

12 Orgel, 'Nobody's Perfect: Or Why Did the English Stage Take Boys for Women?' *South Atlantic Quarterly* 88 (1989), 25.

13 *Flaunting: Style and the Subversive Male Body in Renaissance England*, 2007, p. 78; see pp. 77–102 for Bailey's excellent discussion of the play.

can be tolerated because it can be ignored to something that becomes a sodomitical disorder.

Mortimer's statement that 'this I scorn, that one so basely born' (4.04), a statement that is highlighted by internal rhyme, is largely Marlowe's invention: the historical Gaveston was not of humble origins.[14] While he was not an English nobleman, he had in fact been chosen by Edward I to be the companion of the young prince Edward. Marlowe makes the same changes in status to an even more pronounced degree in the case of Spencer, who becomes Edward's favourite after Gaveston's death. In the play, the younger Spencer is introduced in Scene 5 with Baldock as a retainer of the Earl of Gloucester. Spencer was actually from a noble British family – his father was a baron and Spencer himself was the first cousin of the Earl of Warwick, who features in the play as one of Gaveston's primary opponents – and he had married Edward II's niece (the sister of Gaveston's wife) in the lifetime of Edward I and long before he became Edward's favourite. Clearly, Marlowe wished to create a collision between Edward's choice of lovers and the English class system when in fact none really existed. Because of these changes, the Gaveston and Spencer of *Edward II* come to resemble Marlowe himself, the shoemaker's son who used scholarship to rise above his original status.

A similar point can be made about Gaveston's foreignness. At various points in the play, the fact that he is French is mentioned disapprovingly, and he is associated with other foreign countries as well.[15] It is true that Gaveston's family was from Gascony in southern France, but he had spent most of his life in England and this was in any case a period in which the distinction between England and France (and especially those parts of France under English control, as Gascony was for most of Edward's life) was not so clear cut as it was in Marlowe's time. The other important French character in the play is of course Isabella, and the contrast between her and Gaveston in this regard is instructive. When the Earl of Lancaster sees Isabella bewailing her unhappy state early on in the play, for example, he says to his fellow nobles 'Look where the sister of the King of France / Sits wringing of her hands and beats her breast' (4.187–8).[16] Isabella's foreignness is an asset: her marriage to Edward cemented an alliance between the countries and, as Lancaster's statement could be taken to imply, her mistreatment could lead to war between the countries.

---

14 A good account of Gaveston's background can be found in J.S. Hamilton, *Piers Gaveston, Earl of Cornwall 1307–1312: Politics and Patronage in the Reign of Edward II*, 1988, pp. 19–28.

15 For a discussion of the association of Gaveston with Italy, see Bailey, *Flaunting*, p. 97 *et seq.* For his association with Ireland, see Marcie Bianco, 'To Sodomize a Nation: *Edward II*, Ireland, and the Threat of Penetration,' *Early Modern Literary Studies* 16 (October 2007).

16 Similarly, Lancaster later refers to her as 'Thy gentle Queen, sole sister to Valois' (6.169).

The parallels between Gaveston and Isabella are most concisely demonstrated in an exchange that takes place a little earlier in the fourth scene:

ISABELLA
Villain, 'tis thou that robb'st me of my lord.
GAVESTON
Madam, 'tis you that rob me of my lord.   (4.160–1)

In juxtaposing these two similar yet antithetical statements, Marlowe forces us to consider how we evaluate relationships.[17] Both statements could be said to be correct: although Isabella and Edward are of course legally married, Gaveston has the prior claim – he had been Edward's companion since 1298, while Edward and Isabella were not married until 1308 – and he is clearly the one Edward prefers. This exchange encapsulates what is most transgressive about Marlowe's play, which is not that the king has a favourite with whom he commits sodomy, but rather that he seeks to give this favourite the status of a consort. Edward's attempts to make Gaveston into his consort represent the ultimate point of collision between his private and public lives. The nobles move against the king because he seeks to make his 'wanton humour' into a political fact or, as we would say now, a same-sex marriage.

Nevertheless, it is important to acknowledge that although Gaveston acts as a transgressive element in the world of the play, this transgression would not entail a total reformulation of English society. For instance, when Gaveston says 'Base leaden earls that glory in your birth, / Go sit at home and eat your tenants' beef' (6.74–5), he makes a valid and potentially radical point about the fact that noble status is conferred primarily by material possessions rather than by birth, but his exposure of what we could call the cattle nexus, on the model of Marx and Engels's description of the cash nexus that subtends the class system, should not be taken to indicate that he is a proto-Marxist. Instead, Gaveston, like Baldock later and, presumably, like Marlowe himself, feels that wealth and position are things that a man should be capable of acquiring rather than merely inheriting. Gaveston's desire is to be at the top of the hierarchy, rather than to do away with the hierarchy altogether.[18]

---

17 A brief but interesting discussion of this and other antithetical statements in *Edward II* is in Judith Haber, *Desire and Dramatic Form in Early Modern England*, 2009, p. 29.

18 An excellent discussion of the limits of the transgressive potential of sodomy in the play can be found in Dympna Callaghan, 'The Terms of Gender: "Gay" and "Feminist" *Edward II*', in *Feminist Readings of Early Modern Culture: Emerging Subjects*, ed. Valerie Traub, M. Lindsay Kaplan, and Dympna Callaghan, 1996, pp. 275–301; see especially pp. 283–4.

Gaveston's eye to the main chance is apparent from the play's opening lines, as he reads a letter from Edward:

> 'My father is deceased; come Gaveston,
> And share the kingdom with thy dearest friend.'
> Ah, words that make me surfeit with delight!
> What greater bliss can hap to Gaveston,
> Than live and be the favourite of a king?
> Sweet prince, I come   (1.1–6)

In any edition of the play, the speech prefix, the stage directions, and the punctuation all make it clear that Gaveston is the one speaking; in performance, however, it would not be entirely clear until the beginning of the sixth line that the speaker is Gaveston reading a letter he has received rather than Edward reading a letter he is about to send. Although this confusion between Edward and Gaveston is only temporary, it should lead us to consider that if Gaveston feels that he has the right to the same status as the nobles he may also feel that he has the right to the same status as the king, a point that is borne out by his frequent assumption of command. Perhaps Gaveston seeks not only to be the king's consort, but also to replace him altogether.

In any case, Gaveston certainly seeks to control the king. In the second of his two great soliloquies at the beginning of the play, he rejects the service of the men who have approached him and declares his need for wanton poets, pleasant wits,

> Musicians, that with touching of a string
> May draw the pliant King which way I please. (1.50–2)

Since, as he goes on to say, 'Music and poetry' (1.53) are what Edward likes, he can use these aesthetic pleasures to control Edward for his own advantage. And when Gaveston uses the indefinite article to refer to Edward – as he does in the passage quoted above when he says 'to be the favourite of *a* king' (emphasis added) – he reveals that whatever his feelings may be for Edward as a man, his primary interest is in self-advancement.

The aesthetic pleasures Gaveston plans are also sexual and theatrical, as he makes clear when he says that 'Like sylvan nymphs my pages shall be clad' (1.57) and, especially, when he envisages

> a lovely boy in Dian's shape,
> With hair that gilds the water as it glides,
> Crownets of pearl about his naked arms,

And in his sportful hands an olive tree
To hide those parts which men delight to see (1.60–4)[19]

But Gaveston's vision of a transvestite eroticism is not itself sodomitical, strictly speaking. In implying that the 'parts which men delight to see' are male rather than female genitals, he makes a metatheatrical point that makes perfect sense in a theatre in which all female parts, as it were, were played by male actors. In the world of the Elizabethan theatre, male hetero-erotic desire is inescapably homoerotic. It is noteworthy that we never see anything resembling Gaveston's planned masque in *Edward II*: the only transvestites we see are Isabella and Gaveston's wife, the play's only female characters. What is sodomitical (in the sense of posing a threat to the social order) in Gaveston's speech is that homoeroticism is not presented as marginal or alternative, but rather as the truth of sexual behaviour.

Here, as elsewhere in the play, Gaveston is presented as being more honest than most or even all of the other characters. It is partly this honesty that makes him arguably the most vivid character in the play. The comparison between him and Spencer, his replacement as the king's favourite, is not to the latter's advantage, but they are not the only sodomites in the play. Keeping in mind that in the Renaissance sodomy indicated a general social disorder rather than only a specific sexual act, we can see that both Isabella and Mortimer are – or, at least, become – sodomites.[20] Such a label may seem unlikely in the case of Isabella, the king's legal wife and the woman who embodies the bond between England and France and thus serves to underwrite the social order that sodomy threatens, but over the course of the play she changes from being a wronged wife to being instru-mental in bringing about a civil war that results in her husband's murder and, temporarily, the concentration of royal power in the person of her lover Mortimer, who, as a noble, has no title to rule England.

Most critics have felt that Isabella is a loyal and loving wife in the first half of the play and that her emergence as the she-wolf of France is dramat-ically implausible, but as Claude J. Summers pointed out forty years ago it is clearly she who comes up with the idea that if Gaveston is recalled from exile he can be killed.[21] As the nobles discuss their hatred for Gaveston in

---

19 For an excellent discussion of this scene, see Jonathan Goldberg, *Sodometries: Renaissance Texts, Modern Sexualities*, 1992, pp. 114–15.

20 For a discussion of Mortimer as a sodomite, see Mario DiGangi, *The Homoerotics of Early Modern Drama*, 1997, especially p. 114.

21 Summers, 'Isabella's Plea for Gaveston in Marlowe's *Edward II*,' *Philological Quarterly* 52 (1973), 309. For a perceptive analysis of Isabella in the context of Marlowe's female characters, see Gibbs, 'Marlowe's Politic Women,' in *Constructing Christopher Marlowe*, ed. J.A. Downie and J.T. Parnell, 2000, 164–70.

the fourth scene, Isabella and Mortimer stand apart and talk; when they rejoin the nobles Mortimer announces the plan. While Gaveston has already hinted that Isabella loves Mortimer (4.147–8, when she denies the accusation), this is the audience's first indication that there may be a covert association between them. The conspiring they do in this scene turns out to be paradigmatic of their behaviour for the rest of the play, and begins the process that will end with Edward's murder. Trading on her legitimate position within the social hierarchy (a position that is intended to secure both domestic and foreign order) and, explicitly and repeatedly, on her position as wife of the present king and mother of the future king, Isabella brings about one of the most serious challenges to the social order in all of medieval English history.

In her career as a sodomite, Isabella is of course largely under the control of her lover Mortimer. It is Mortimer who emerges as the most sodomitical character in the play, and although he is ultimately executed, for most of the second half of the play he is more successful and infinitely more powerful than either Gaveston or Spencer ever was. *Edward II* could be said to be based, at least initially, on a pair of binary oppositions – Edward–Gaveston and Isabella–Mortimer – in each case, a monarch and his or her favourite. But although we might feel that heterosexual behaviour is always more licit than homosexual behaviour, in the context of a royal married couple when the sovereign is male his sexual infidelities can usually be accommodated, which is part of the point that the elder Mortimer makes to his nephew. On the other hand, the sexual infidelity of the queen, with its potential to undermine the absolute reliance on patrilineal descent that is necessary to royal succession, can only be seen as a threat. While this issue never explicitly emerges in *Edward II*, it is impossible to believe that it would not have occurred to Marlowe or his audience.

From this point of view, then, Mortimer poses a danger to the basis of the English monarchy in a way that Gaveston cannot. The play as a whole, especially its second half, documents the extent to which Mortimer plays the sodomite in his challenge to and reformulation of the social order on which medieval England depended. Furthermore, just as Edward's transgression lies in his seeking to elevate Gaveston to the level of a consort, so too the behaviour of Isabella and Mortimer demonstrates that the threat to the social order that is called sodomy is not restricted to male–male sexual relations. Rather than presenting Edward and Gaveston as somehow separate from the world in which they live, or presenting what we now call male homosexuality as different, Marlowe demonstrates that heterosexual attachments can also be sodomitical.

Audience Sympathy

The issue of where the audience's sympathies lie – and how they change over the course of the play – is an important aspect of the criticism of any play, and perhaps especially of any play that can be considered to be a tragedy, despite the fact that it is never really possible to speak of the audience as a homogeneous group. When critics speak of the audience's sympathy they are often really speaking about their own sympathies and biases, which may or may not be the same as any given audience's. Furthermore, sympathies are often influenced by the way in which the play is presented. In the case of a live production, the presentation may include performance, costuming, blocking, and so on. In the case of a play that is read, the presentation chiefly consists of the introduction, although the glosses and marginal notes can also be influential. These comments may all seem obvious, but part of what is most insidious about the ideological work done by critics is that audience sympathies are presumed to be something about which a critic may speak with absolute confidence, so I have thought it best to address the question specifically (and, of course, tendentiously).

The question of audience sympathies has been especially vexed in the case of *Edward II*, as discussions of the audience's reaction to the play have intersected with highly emotive views on sexuality. The consensus among critics writing on *Edward II* has been that the audience sides with Isabella and, to a lesser extent, with the nobles for the first half of the play, and then with Edward for the second half. The consensus has also been that no character in the play reaches the status of a true tragic hero: Edward is too weak, and both Gaveston and Mortimer are too self-serving. For these reasons, it has often been useful for critics to consider *Edward II* primarily as a history play in which, for the most part, no characters are expected to be truly tragic.

Another way to classify the play's genre, and one that would significantly affect the question of audience reaction, is to analyse the play as a romantic tragedy.[22] From this point of view, the audience's sympathies would be expected to lie with Edward and Gaveston, just as they are expected to lie with Romeo and Juliet. This view of the play has really only emerged as an interpretive possibility in approximately the last quarter-century, however, and in this section I shall chiefly be concerned with the standard factors that have been felt to influence the audience's reactions to the play.

22 One of the few critics to consider this approach is Leonora Leet Brodwin, but she stepped back from the brink: 'I have excluded Marlowe's great history play from this study, however, because it cannot be considered exclusively as a love tragedy' (*Elizabethan Love Tragedy, 1587–1625*, 1971, p. 383 n. 5). This statement is also true of all of the plays Brodwin does discuss, but as those plays focus on heteroeroticism she was apparently willing to overlook that fact.

I am interested both in the way discussions of how the audience feels are connected to ideas about sexuality and in the way these discussions are connected to ideas about kingship.

The homophobia that has dominated critical discussions of *Edward II* has resulted in the consensus that Edward, as an unfaithful husband, as a sodomite, and as a weak king could not be a sympathetic character until he is deposed, degraded, imprisoned, and finally and horribly murdered. In his dreadful downfall, that is, Edward becomes legible as the character whose sins (in his case, homosexuality) can be pardoned because he is punished by death.[23] From this perspective Edward resembles, for instance, Annabella in John Ford's *'Tis Pity She's a Whore* (first published in 1633), the willing perpetrator of incest who achieves a tragic grandeur in her horrible death. On the other hand, many critics writing more recently have had no problems with sodomy itself and have been inclined to sympathize with a character they consider to be the victim of vicious homophobia.

A reading of the play that is sympathetic to homosexuality is useful in a time like the present, in which vicious homophobia still exists. But this is not only a presentist approach (that is, this approach does not privilege the present over the past); instead, it is warranted by the extent to which Marlowe, as I have shown, seeks to present Edward's love for Gaveston as at least as legitimate as his marriage to Isabella. But there are other ways in which Marlowe also seeks to arouse sympathy for Edward and Gaveston. One obvious example occurs in the play's first scene, when the Bishop of Coventry declares his enmity to Gaveston. Edward assaults Coventry, at which point the Earl of Kent intervenes:

KENT
    Ah brother, lay not violent hands on him,
    For he'll complain unto the See of Rome.
GAVESTON
    Let him complain unto the See of Hell.   (1.188–90)

It has often been assumed that Marlowe's audience would have objected to this rough handling of a priest, but surely a Protestant audience in the late sixteenth century would have relished the linking of Rome with Hell. When the Bishop of Canterbury sends a messenger to appeal to the Pope (2.35–8), it is impossible not to believe that the English public, so soon after the Armada, in which a Catholic monarch sought and obtained the

---

23 The idea that a character's homosexuality can be at least partially excused if he or she is ultimately killed has been the basis of many recent analyses of plays and (especially) films; the most famous discussion is Vito Russo, *The Celluloid Closet: Homosexuality in the Movies*, 1987.

Pope's support for an invasion of England, would have been disposed to consider Edward a champion of English liberty, a point that is underlined in the fourth scene when Edward, in one of his few soliloquies, addresses 'Proud Rome' (4.97) and threatens to 'fire thy crazèd buildings and enforce / The papal towers to kiss the lowly ground' (4.100–1).[24]

Suggesting that an Elizabethan audience would have enjoyed anti-Catholicism and an articulation of English nationalism is hardly controversial. Suggesting that any audience would have felt sorry for a man tormented and horribly murdered, however much they might have objected to his earlier life, should not be controversial, although it would be no exaggeration to say that much of the criticism on Edward's death is characterized by sadism. Now, at least, both these means of arousing sympathy for Edward seem fairly obvious. What does not seem so obvious is suggesting that Edward should not necessarily be considered a weak king, although he is undeniably an unorthodox one. After all, the 'weak king' label has been very useful for critics, allowing them to link *Edward II* to *Richard II* just as, for example, *The Jew of Malta* is often linked to *The Merchant of Venice* and *Dido, Queen of Carthage* to *Antony and Cleopatra*. (This is as good a place as any to comment that the literary critics' favourite male–male couple, at least in the Renaissance, is Marlowe and Shakespeare.) And it is important to point out that in declaring Edward to have been a weak king, literary critics fall in line with the consensus among historians, according to which Edward's failures as a king were both considerable in themselves and especially noticeable because of the contrasts with both his father and his son.

Edward is considered to be a weak king chiefly because of his lack of interest in the military matters that so preoccupied both his father and his son and that were felt to be central to the role of the king. The opposition between Edward and war is first hinted at near the play's beginning, when a soldier seeks employment from Gaveston only to be told that 'I have no war, and therefore, sir, be gone' (1.35). It is typical of the play that it is Gaveston rather than Edward who introduces this theme. Marlowe repeatedly demonstrates the extent to which it is Gaveston who dominates the king, rather than the other way around. In this respect, Edward is certainly a weak king, and his subordination to his favourite may well be intended as a tacit comment on Henry III of France's excessive reliance on his favourites and even on Queen Elizabeth herself.[25]

---

24 One of the few critical discussions of Catholicism in *Edward II* is Chloe Kathleen Preedy, *Marlowe's Literary Skepticism: Politic Religion and Post-Restoration Polemic*, 2012, pp. 136-41.

25 The best commentator on the relationship between *Edward II* and the politics of Marlowe's day is Curtis Perry; see note 6 above.

Accusations of Edward's lack of interest in war can be found throughout the play, but perhaps the best examples come from the sixth scene, in which the nobles first openly threaten civil war to the king's face. Mortimer declares that

> The idle triumphs, masques, lascivious shows,
> And prodigal gifts bestowed on Gaveston
> Have drawn thy treasure dry and made thee weak (6.154–6)

Lancaster follows by referring to recent defeats in France and to rebellions in Ireland and Scotland, and Mortimer speaks again to lament the domination of the Danes in the North Sea. They find much else to criticize about Edward (including his treatment of Isabella) and Lancaster goes so far as to threaten both rebellion and deposition (6.158), but return to English defeats in Scotland, most notable of which was the ignominious defeat at Bannockburn in 1314, after which they storm out, threatening to return armed for civil war.

Interestingly, in the midst of this enumeration of recent disasters in English military affairs, Mortimer finds time to speak critically of what he claims was Edward's only appearance as a soldier:

> then thy soldiers marched like players,
> With garish robes, not armour; and thyself,
> Bedaubed with gold, rode laughing at the rest,
> Nodding and shaking of thy spangled crest
> Where women's favours hung like labels down. (6.180–4)

As so often, Mortimer is talking about clothing, but what is most significant about his speech is its direct juxtaposition of war with two kinds of theatre – both plays, since the soldiers are like actors, and tournaments, as Edward appears not as a man preparing to fight but rather as a man preparing for a tournament – that is, for a highly theatrical version of conflict. In Mortimer's opinion, Edward cannot be a king: he can only act the role of a king and he is not even convincing in his performance of this role.

Most critics have accepted Mortimer's and his fellow nobles' assessment of Edward's reign and have judged him deficient as a king, but we are not obliged to do so. Is it the purpose of a king to effect the greatest possible slaughter of foreigners? Is it the purpose of a king to ensure the subjugation of foreign countries? There are not rhetorical questions. Tamburlaine would certainly have given both questions a very enthusiastic assent, and the campaigns of Edward I and Edward III demonstrate that they would have agreed with him, but we should at least entertain the possibility that Marlowe might have wanted us to consider that there are other ways to be a king. Even in Marlowe's own time, when England was frequently under threat of various kinds from foreign powers, it is surely not inconceivable that an audience that had paid money to see a play might prefer plays to genocide. The events of the play seem to endorse the view that Edward is a weak king, as he is first forced to abdicate and then murdered, but there is surely no reason why we should side with the nobles merely because they are successful.

What is more, the almost unanimous consensus among contemporary critics that Edward was a weak king is simply bizarre, as contemporary critics do not, presumably, support the violent subjugation of the Irish, Scottish, and French. Nor can we excuse accepting the views of man like Mortimer on what kingship should be merely on the grounds that this was the majority opinion in either the early fourteenth century or the late fifteenth century. A host of feminist and queer analyses (to name only two kinds of politically engaged criticism) of literature from earlier periods has started from the assumption that neither a contemporary critic nor a writer from long ago is obliged to accept the dominant prejudices of the day. Perhaps we should consider that Marlowe, whose plays and poems present an exceptionally wide variety of radical opinions, might want us to sympathize with a king who would rather spend the country's money on culture than on killing.

Marlovian Aspects

The adjective 'Marlovian' is generally taken to mean two things: a main character who seeks to transcend his beginnings and gain more power (Tamburlaine and the Duke of Guise) or more knowledge (Faustus) or more money (Barabas); and powerful and elevated verse. Judged from this point of view, *Edward II* has seemed insufficiently Marlovian. The language of the play is, for the most part, relatively prosaic, especially compared to either *Tamburlaine* or *Dr Faustus*. Some time ago, M.C. Bradbrook wrote that '*Edward II* is generally acclaimed as Marlowe's greatest dramatic success; but this is only possible by ignoring Elizabethan standards, and judging purely on "construction". As poetic drama, the last speech of Edward is inferior to the last speech of Faustus or even to the early soliloquies of *The Jew of Malta*, and how it is possible to fail as poetry and succeed as drama is not easy to understand.'[26] In his discussion of the play, J.B. Steane quoted Bradbrook's comments and added that 'the verse is

26 Bradbrook, *Themes and Conventions of Elizabethan Tragedy*, 1957, pp. 160–1.

indeed normally thin and drab. Gaveston's first speech is fine, but generally it is a matter of only lines and phrases here and there having any considerable poetic merit.'[27]

These comments may seem old-fashioned, but it is undeniable that *Edward II* is not an especially poetic play. One reason for this can be found in Steane's comment that 'Gaveston's first speech is fine'. Most of the poetic interest in the play does indeed come from Gaveston, and mostly from his opening soliloquies. Another way to put this is to say that the play opens with a display of Marlowe's poetic powers – a display that the audience would have expected – but then becomes prosaic. There are flashes of poetic power throughout the play, but the dialogue tends to be matter-of-fact. We can regard this too as an attempt to get the audience to be sympathetic to Gaveston, since he provides the bulk of what the audience had learnt to understand as Marlovian language. His importance to the play can also be found in the fact that, as Susan McCloskey pointed out, 'references in the text . . . indicate that all the scenes in Acts I and II occur in the daytime. After Gaveston's death in Act III, darkness descends over nearly half the scenes.'[28] Marlowe makes Gaveston essential to the play's setting and language in order to demonstrate the importance of the aesthetic element even in a history play. In the world of the play, those who see Gaveston as an evil to be defeated must accept the consequences of a darkened stage with mainly prosaic language.

An especially good example of the attitude to language in the play (or, at least, in the second half of the play) comes when Isabella returns to England at the head of an army. She begins an elaborate speech, replete with generalizations about civil war and a denunciation of Edward. At the beginning of the fourteenth line of the speech, Mortimer interrupts her and says 'madam, if you be a warrior, / Ye must not grow so passionate in speeches' (17.14–15). He then gives a short, clear, and poetically undistinguished summary of their views, and the scene closes with the trumpets announcing the forward march – a shift from verbal to non-verbal signifiers. Although Mortimer himself shows at times a real gift for rhetoric and has some very good lines, his intervention here is paradigmatic of a preference for action over language that comes to dominate the play, at the expense of the stirring rhetoric that is characteristic of a play such as *Tamburlaine* throughout. In *Edward II*, this rhetoric is almost exclusively the province of Gaveston, and once he is killed, poetic language itself becomes associated with what Mortimer and the peers see as a 'wanton humour' that threatens to destroy the status quo.

27 Steane, *Marlowe: A Critical Study*, 1964, p. 207.
28 McCloskey, 'The Worlds of *Edward II*', *Renaissance Drama* n.s. 16 (1985), 40.

The language of *Edward II* is, of course, only prosaic in the specialized sense of not being as grand as Marlowe's usual language. We can point to Edward's 'But what are kings, when regiment is gone, / But perfect shadows in a sunshine day?' (20.26–7), and it is clearly the case that Edward becomes increasingly poetic as his death approaches.[29] The play also affords a number of examples of a certain kind of humour, as when the distraught Edward bids farewell to Gaveston, who is about to go into exile:

GAVESTON
    'Tis something to be pitied of a king.
EDWARD
    Thou shalt not hence; I'll hide thee, Gaveston.
GAVESTON
    I shall be found, and then 'twill grieve me more. (4.130–2)

Gaveston's hard-headed and realistic attitude here and elsewhere (as in the retort to the nobles about their tenant's beef quoted above) are attractive, and recall the grim humour that is so salient a feature of *The Jew of Malta*, for instance. In this sense, it is not that *Edward II* is not Marlovian, but rather that our sense of what it means to be Marlovian is unduly limited.

The general understanding of a Marlovian character is also somewhat restrictive. We tend to feel that the typical Marlovian character is, as Harry Levin pointed out sixty years ago, an 'overreacher', a character who always wants more of the world's wealth and power.[30] Considered in this regard, Edward, who shows no interest in enlarging his kingdom or extending his power, can only be a disappointment. But Edward does resemble Dido, the star of Marlowe's play *Dido, Queen of Carthage*. Both are monarchs, which is to say that they already have the wealth and power that a character like Tamburlaine desires, but both seek a private happiness for which they are prepared to sacrifice almost everything. When Edward says

    Make several kingdoms of this monarchy,
    And share it equally amongst you all,
    So I may have some nook or corner left
    To frolic with my dearest Gaveston. (4.70–3)

he expresses a sentiment which Dido would share. We could say that these Marlovian characters want less, rather than more.

---

29 Nevertheless, he has few of the big moments one might expect. As William B. Kelly points out, Edward has very few soliloquies (and even fewer long soliloquies); see Kelly, 'Mapping Subjects in Marlowe's *Edward II*', *South Atlantic Quarterly* 63.1 (1998), 5.

30 See Levin, *The Overreacher: A Study of Christopher Marlowe*, 1952. This is still one of the best monographs on Marlowe.

On the other hand, both Gaveston and Mortimer, in their constant striving for more power, do resemble a character like Tamburlaine. Certainly, Mortimer's last lines strike a note of real tragic grandeur (rather than mere pathos, which predominates in Edward's final scenes):

> Farewell, fair Queen. Weep not for Mortimer,
> That scorns the world, and as a traveller
> Goes to discover countries yet unknown.   (25.64–6)

The grandeur is qualified, however, by the fact that Mortimer has been a rather low-grade character throughout, with none of Tamburlaine's undeniable charisma. As well, Marlowe in effect gives Gaveston the first half of the play and Mortimer the second, an indication that neither is sufficient to dominate the play in the way that Faustus or Tamburlaine dominated theirs. The world in which *Edward II* takes place is apparently unable to support the larger-than-life characters that we have come to see as typically 'Marlovian'.

Conclusion

Once Edward is murdered, the play rapidly comes to its end. It is typical of the play that Mortimer orders the murder by sending an ambiguous message (in Latin: '*Edwardum occidere nolite timere bonum est*'), one that – depending on the punctuation – means either 'Do not kill the king, it is good to fear' or 'Do not fear, it is good to kill the king.' Judith Haber has argued that this lack of a clear meaning is typical of the play and that not only Mortimer but also Gaveston are always trying 'to manipulate and control indeterminacy'.[31] In *Edward II*, language is not something that has an illocutionary force, as it arguably does in *Tamburlaine*, but rather something that is inherently ambiguous. The same statement could be made of the manner in which Edward is murdered, as the insertion of a red-hot poker into the anus will not leave visible marks (or so the theory goes). Even in his death, then, Edward might continue to represent – in fact, literally to embody – the ambiguity and indeterminacy that have characterized so much of the play.

The important word in the last sentence is 'might': the conclusion of *Edward II* effectively shuts down the possibility of change in the world in which the play takes place. In his excellent discussion of the play, Jonathan Goldberg argues that 'the king, from his opening words . . . institutes a

---

31 Haber, *Desire and Dramatic Form*, p. 34. For a similar argument, see Preedy, *Marlowe's Literary Skepticism*, pp. 55–60.

sodomitical regime'.[32] It is not entirely clear what this sodomitical regime would look like, although it would presumably include a focus on aesthetic values rather than military ones (as Edward's priorities indicate), but is clear that this regime is over by the end of the play. For one thing, it ends as it begins, with the death of a king. The circularity is itself significant, as it models the extent to which nothing has changed. We are accustomed to seeing patrilineal succession as teleological and as premised on what Lee Edelman has called 'reproductive futurity', but in this case it appears that what the replacement of one Edward by another represents is not a forward motion but rather an endless loop.[33]

While both the beginning and the ending of the play feature the death of one Edward and the ascension to the throne of another Edward, there are, of course, important differences. At the beginning, the dead king is replaced, not by his son, or rather not just by his son, but by a male couple composed of his son and Gaveston. In addition, the living and the dead kings are only present textually: Edward II through the letter he has written to Gaveston and Edward I through his mention in that letter. And, as pointed out earlier, the play's beginning is ambiguous in that it is not at first clear who is speaking. The beginning might thus seem to introduce the audience to a world of homoeroticism, ambiguity, and textuality, and the letter Gaveston holds could be said to represent the aesthetic pleasures he plans for the king.

At the play's conclusion, many of these features are present but in a new form. For instance, the ambiguity of the play's beginning – an ambiguity that is present through much of the play – changes into the unambiguous letter with which Mortimer orders the king's death. Because of its lack of punctuation, the letter is designed to appear ambiguous, but the ambiguity is only superficial. It is understood as a warrant to murder the king, both by the men who carry out the order and by Edward III himself, who presents the letter as proof of Mortimer's guilt in the final scene. Marlowe also effects two very important substitutions in what we could see as his recension of the first scene at the end of the play. The homoerotic male couple of Edward and Gaveston is replaced both by the homosocial male couple of father and son (a bond that had been denied by the flouting of the last king's wishes with which the play begins) and by the male couple of the murdered king and the man who ordered his murder, as Mortimer's severed head is intended to decorate the top of Edward's coffin.[34]

---

32 Goldberg, *Sodometries*, p. 123.

33 See Edelman, *No Future: Queer Theory and the Death Drive*, 2004, especially pp. 1–31.

34 Marlowe's connection of Edward's hearse and Mortimer's head is unhistorical, as Edward was murdered in 1327 and Mortimer was not executed until the end of 1330.

Both the similarity and the difference of the play's beginning and ending can perhaps most succinctly be demonstrated by juxtaposing Gaveston's ardent and romantic 'Sweet prince' (1.6) – the phrase is especially marked since, as pointed out, this is the moment at which the identity of the speaker first becomes clear – with Edward III's lachrymose 'Sweet father' (25.99), spoken to his father's hearse. In fact, 'Sweet prince' may have been particularly resonant for Marlowe's contemporary audience, since, as Jeffrey Masten has demonstrated, the adjective 'sweet' was often used in the Renaissance to express love between men.[35] We could sum up *Edward II* by saying that the play describes the trajectory from 'sweet' as a word that emphasizes a homoerotic bond and 'sweet' as a word that expresses a conventional familial piety. Edward III has avenged his father, but the repetitions of the play's conclusion signal the reestablishment of the old order and, in effect, the elision of Edward II.[36] The possibilities for a different way of life that Edward represented, however partially and imperfectly, are shut out in favour of a tyrannical continuity.

STEPHEN GUY-BRAY

---

35 See Masten, 'Toward a Queer Address: The Taste of Letters and Early Modern Male Friendship,' *GLQ* 10.3, (2004), 367–84, especially 378, where Masten specifically discusses Gaveston's use of 'Sweet prince.'
36 For a particularly grim version of this argument, see John F. McElroy, 'Repetition, Contrariety, and Individualization in *Edward II*', *Studies in English Literature* 24 (1984), 205–24, especially 211.

NOTE ON THE TEXT

The control-text for this edition is the 1594 octavo, the earliest and only authoritative edition of *Edward II*, which was probably printed from an authorial manuscript. It is a particularly rare book: only one copy survives, and is held by the Zentralbibliothek, Zürich, Switzerland; a second copy, incorporating some uncorrected formes, was in existence in the Landes-bibliothek, Cassel, Germany, until it was destroyed by bombing during the Second World War. Although the edition was printed in octavo format, it has the general appearance of a quarto, and the editors have adopted the traditional practice of referring to it as Q.

Subsequent editions were printed in 1598, 1612, and 1622 (Q2–4 respectively), but these are of limited interest: in each case the compositors sought to improve the punctuation and spelling of Q, as well as introducing a number of their own inauthoritative readings. There are also a number of peculiar and unlikely variants in a manuscript version of the first seventy lines of the play, in the Dyce collection at the Victoria and Albert Museum, London. Produced to replace the first two leaves of a quarto, this is dated 1593, and so purports to be the earliest surviving text of *Edward II*. Recent scholarship, however, has shown that the manuscript was probably prepared by a scribe copying from Q.

Q presents the editor with a number of technical problems: stage directions are often missing or wrongly positioned, speech prefixes are inconsistent, and there are a number of compositorial bungles. In this edition, the punctuation has been silently altered where necessary and speech prefixes have been regularized. All significant changes to the lineation of verse are recorded in the notes; however, changes to the division of prose passages and verse lines split to accommodate them within the physical dimensions of Q are not recorded. The spelling has been modernized throughout according to the principles set down by Stanley Wells in his *Modernizing Shakespeare's Spelling* (Oxford, 1979); a few interesting cases where the old form differs significantly from the modern are recorded in the notes. Proper names have also been silently modernized, so that, for example, 'Matrevis' becomes Maltravers, 'Gurney' becomes Gourney, and 'Bartley' becomes Berkeley.

One such modernization, of 'Killingworth' to Kenilworth, raises difficult issues. The name can be taken to combine geographical precision with an undertone foreshadowing Edward's eventual fate; this means that the modernizing editor is faced with two options, neither of which preserves the full original effect. Each, moreover, has particular disadvantages of its own: to retain 'Killingworth' in an otherwise fully modernized edition is implicitly, and erroneously, to move the location several hundred miles, to the castleless Tyneside village now famous for its associations with George Stephenson; while the name of Kenilworth has picked up irrelevant romantic connotations from Sir Walter Scott's novel of that title (1821). Besides consistency with the editors' practice elsewhere in the edition, the case for modernization turns on the primacy of the geographical reference, whereas the suggestion of killing is only a *potential* pun, a secondary meaning probably, but not necessarily, intended by the author.[1] The spelling 'Killingworth' is simply the form of the name used by Holinshed and retained by Marlowe: there is no positive evidence that he deliberately adopted it for literary effect. In point of fact, no killing takes place at 'Killingworth': Edward is moved to Berkeley before he is murdered (21.60). It is not, then, an ironic name for Edward's final destination, like the King's Jerusalem chamber in Shakespeare's *Henry IV, Part 2*. Moreover, there is no point at which the characters seem aware that 'Killingworth' is anything other than a place name. While the editors believe that a secondary meaning is present, creating for the audience a generalized ominous effect, this remains a matter of critical inference rather than demonstrable textual fact. Accordingly, the modernized form 'Kenilworth' is adopted in this edition.

In the treatment of stage directions, the editors have been concerned to balance fidelity to the written text with the need to convey to a reader something of the experience of seeing the play in the theatre. Q's Latin directions have been silently translated, with the exception of '*Exit*' and '*Exeunt*', and square brackets have been used to denote directions (or parts thereof) supplied by the editors. A number of directions to enter are given late in Q, presumably to indicate the point at which the characters concerned enter the action rather than the stage; the editors have repositioned such directions to indicate the point at which those characters become visible to a theatre audience, and sometimes to other characters already on stage.

There are numerous inconsistencies in the designation of characters in stage directions and speech prefixes: Edward is also 'King', Isabella is also 'Queen', Kent is also 'Edmund', and so on. The most textually important of these inconsistencies concerns Maltravers, who is first introduced as the Earl of Arundel in Scene 9, but who is most frequently referred to as 'Matrevis', even in the dialogue. Since Arundel and Maltravers were distinct historical persons, editors have usually supposed these references in Scenes 9, 11, and 16 to be erroneous, and have treated 'Arundel' as a separate character

1   Cf. Stanley Wells, *Modernizing Shakespeare's Spelling* (Oxford, 1979), pp. 10–12

from 'Matrevis' who appears in Scenes 21, 22, 24, and 25; the error was explained by the hypothesis that Marlowe had intended the two roles to be doubled, and had confused their names accordingly. This edition, however, presupposes that there is no textual error and that Q's 'Arundel' and 'Matrevis' are simply variant ways of designating a single character. Marlowe was probably influenced by the fact that the later Earls of Arundel also held the title Lord Maltravers; it was not the only occasion on which his treatment of the fourteenth-century barons was affected by the heraldry of his own time.[2]

Q contains no act- or scene-divisions. In 1818, James Broughton introduced a five-act structure which has been adopted (with some variations) in most subsequent editions.[3] Such a structure was recognized in Marlowe's time as a literary device, and some plays (including *The Comedy of Errors* and *Henry V*) were written in five acts. There is no evidence that this was the case with *Edward II*, however. Moreover, until 1608 at the earliest, act-divisions were not used in the open-air theatres for which *Edward II* was written: plays were performed continuously from the first scene to the last. The editors have, accordingly, chosen to divide the play only into its scenes, the better to represent its original impact in the theatre.

Although this edition departs from the editorial tradition in several significant respects, the editors' debt to their predecessors remains substantial. The play's first named editor was Robert Dodsley, who included it in his multi-volume collection of *Old Plays* in 1744. The nineteenth century saw the evolution of interventionist editing, and some of the principal textual hypotheses, still accepted by recent editors, were tentatively formulated by Alexander Dyce in 1850 (in *The Works of Christopher Marlowe*, volume 2). In the twentieth century the most important bibliographical work was done in the editions of W.W. Greg (1926) and Fredson Bowers (1973; in *The Complete Works of Christopher Marlowe*, volume 2), while those of H. B. Charlton and R.D. Waller (1933), Charles R. Forker (1994), and Richard Rowland (1994) made especially significant contributions to the play's criticism and exegesis. The editors have also found useful the editions of William Dinsmore Briggs (1914), W. Moelwyn Merchant (1967), Roma Gill (1967), and David Bevington and Eric Rasmussen (in *Doctor Faustus and Other Plays*, 1995).

MARTIN WIGGINS

---

2 See 13.25 n. The hypothesis is presented at greater length in Martin Wiggins, 'Arundel and Maltravers: A Textual Problem in *Edward II*, *N&Q* 242 (1997), 42–7.

3 The commonest division of the play is as follows: Scenes 1–4 = Act 1; Scenes 5–9 = Act 2; Scenes 10–13 = Act 3; Scenes 14–19 = Act 4; Scenes 20–25 = Act 5.

ABBREVIATIONS

Editions of the Play Cited

Bevington and Rasmussen	*Doctor Faustus and Other Plays*, ed. David Bevington and Eric Rasmussen (Oxford, 1995)
Briggs	*Edward II*, ed. William Dinsmore Briggs (London, 1914)
Charlton and Waller	*Edward II*, ed. H.B. Charlton and R.D. Waller (London, 1933)
Forker	*Edward the Second*, ed. Charles R. Forker, The Revels Plays (Manchester and New York, 1994)
Gill	*Edward II*, ed. Roma Gill (London, 1967)
Merchant	*Edward the Second*, ed. W. Moelwyn Merchant, New Mermaids (London, 1967)
Rowland	*The Complete Works of Christopher Marlowe*, vol. III: *Edward II*, ed. Richard Rowland (Oxford, 1994)

Periodicals and Reference Works

Dent	R.W. Dent, *Shakespeare's Proverbial Language: An Index* (Berkeley, 1981)
MLN	*Modern Language Notes*
N&Q	*Notes and Queries*
Tilley	Morris Palmer Tilley (ed.), *A Dictionary of the Proverbs in England in the Sixteenth and Seventeenth Centuries* (Ann Arbor, 1950)

Other plays of Marlowe are quoted from Bevington and Rasmussen and from '*Dido Queen of Carthage*' and '*The Massacre at Paris*', ed. H.J. Oliver, The Revels Plays (London, 1968). Shakespeare is quoted from *The Complete Works*, ed. Stanley Wells, Gary Taylor, John Jowett, and William Montgomery (Oxford, 1986). Other editions quoted are Thomas Lodge, *The Wounds of Civil War*, ed. Joseph W. Houppert, Regents Renaissance Drama (Lincoln, NE, 1969), and George Peele, *Edward I*, ed. Frank S. Hook, in *The Dramatic Works of George Peele*, gen. ed. Charles Tyler Prouty (New Haven and London, 1961).

FURTHER READING

Ahlgren, Angela K. 'Christopher Marlowe's "Unholy Fascination": Performing Queer *Edward II* in the 1990s.' *Journal of Dramatic Theory and Criticism* 25.2 (2011), 5–22.

Armstrong, Raymond. 'More Jiggery than Pokery: Derek Jarman's *Edward II*.' In *British Queer Cinema*, ed. Robin Griffiths. London, 2006, pp. 145–56.

Bailey, Amanda. *Flaunting: Style and the Subversive Male Body in Renaissance England.* Toronto, 2007.

Bartels, Emily C. *Spectacles of Strangeness: Imperialism, Alienation, and Marlowe.* Philadelphia, 1993.

Bianco, Marcie. 'To Sodomize a Nation: *Edward II*, Ireland, and the Threat of Penetration.' *Early Modern Literary Studies* 16 (October 2007).

Bray, Alan. *Homosexuality in Renaissance England.* New York, 1995.

Callaghan, Dympna. 'The Terms of Gender: "Gay" and "Feminist" *Edward II*.' In *Feminist Readings of Early Modern Culture: Emerging Subjects*, ed. Valerie Traub, M. Lindsay Kaplan, and Dympna Callaghan. Cambridge, 1996, pp. 275–301.

DiGangi, Mario. *The Homoerotics of Early Modern Drama.* Cambridge, 1997.

Ellis, Jim. *Derek Jarman's Angelic Conversations.* Minneapolis, 2009.

Fuller, David. 'Love or Politics: The Man or the King?' *Shakespeare Bulletin* 27.1 (2009), 81–115.

Gibbs, Joanna. 'Marlowe's Politic Women.' In *Constructing Christopher Marlowe*, ed. J.A. Downie and J.T. Parnell. Cambridge, 2000, pp. 164–76.

Goldberg, Jonathan. *Sodometries: Renaissance Texts, Modern Sexualities.* Stanford, CA, 1992.

Guy-Bray, Stephen. 'Homophobia and the Depoliticizing of *Edward II*.' *English Studies in Canada* 17 (1991), 125–33.

Haber, Judith. *Desire and Dramatic Form in Early Modern England.* Cambridge, 2009.

Hamilton, J.S. *Piers Gaveston, Earl of Cornwall 1307–1312: Politics and Patronage in the Reign of Edward II.* Detroit, 1988.

Jarman, Derek. *Queer Edward II.* London, 1992.

Kelly, William B. 'Mapping Subjects in Marlowe's *Edward II*.' *South Atlantic Quarterly* 63.1 (1998), 1–19.

Levin, Harry. *The Overreacher: A Study of Christopher Marlowe.* Cambridge, MA, 1952.

MacLure, Millar, ed. *Marlowe: The Critical Heritage, 1588–1896.* London, 1979.

Masten, Jeffrey. 'Toward a Queer Address: The Taste of Letters and Early Modern Male Friendship.' *GLQ* 10.3 (2004), 367–84.

McCloskey, Susan. 'The Worlds of *Edward II.*' *Renaissance Drama* n.s. 16 (1985), 35–48.

McElroy, John F. 'Repetition, Contrariety, and Individualization in *Edward II.*' *Studies in English Literature* 24 (1984), 205–24.

Orgel, Stephen. 'Nobody's Perfect: Or Why Did the English Stage Take Boys for Women?' *South Atlantic Quarterly* 88 (1989), 7–29.

Park, Joan. 'History, Tragedy, and Truth in Christopher Marlowe's *Edward II.*' *Studies in English Literature* 39 (1999), 275–90.

Perry, Curtis. 'The Politics of Access and Representations of the Sodomite King in Early Modern England.' *Renaissance Quarterly* 54 (2000), 1054–83.

Preedy, Chloe Kathleen. *Marlowe's Literary Scepticism: Politic Religion and Post-Restoration Polemic.* London, 2012.

Ryan, Patrick. 'Marlowe's *Edward II* and the Medieval Passion Play.' *Comparative Drama* 32 (1998–99), 465–95.

Shepherd, Simon. *Marlowe and the Politics of Elizabethan Theatre.* Brighton, 1986.

Summers, Claude J. 'Isabella's Plea for Gaveston in Marlowe's *Edward II.*' *Philological Quarterly* 52 (1973), 308–10.

The troublesome

raigne and lamentable death of
Edward *the second, King of*
England: with the tragicall
fall of proud Mortimer:

As it was sundrie times publiquely acted
in the honourable citie of London, by the
right honourable the Earle of Pem-
brooke his seruants.

Written by Chri. Marlow *Gent.*

Imprinted at London for *William Iones,*
dwelling neere Holbourne conduit at the
signe of the Gunne. 1594

DRAMATIS PERSONAE

EDWARD II, *King of England*
ISABELLA, *Queen of England, the King of France's sister*
PRINCE EDWARD, *their son, later King Edward III*
EDMUND, EARL OF KENT, *the King's brother*

THE KING'S FAVOURITES

PIERS GAVESTON, *later Earl of Cornwall*
SPENCER JUNIOR, *Lady Margaret's servant, later Earl of Gloucester*
SPENCER SENIOR, *his father, later Earl of Wiltshire and Marquess of Winchester*
BALDOCK, *a scholar, Lady Margaret's tutor*

THE BARONS

MORTIMER JUNIOR, *of Wigmore*
MORTIMER SENIOR, *of Chirke, his uncle*
THE EARL OF LANCASTER
GUY, EARL OF WARWICK
THE EARL OF PEMBROKE
LORD BEAUMONT
LADY MARGARET DE CLARE, *Gaveston's fiancée*
LORD MALTRAVERS, EARL OF ARUNDEL, *the King's ally, later his keeper*
THE EARL OF LEICESTER
LORD BERKELEY

THE CHURCH

THE BISHOP OF COVENTRY
THE BISHOP OF CANTERBURY
THE ABBOT OF NEATH
MONKS
THE BISHOP OF WINCHESTER

DRAMATIS PERSONAE

THREE POOR MEN
THE CLERK OF THE CROWN
PEMBROKE'S MEN
JAMES, *Pembroke's servant*
A HORSE-BOY, *Pembroke's servant*
LEVUNE, *a Frenchman*
A HERALD
SIR JOHN OF HAINAULT, *the Queen's ally*
RHYS AP HOWELL
THE MAYOR OF BRISTOL
A MOWER
TRUSSEL, *a representative of Parliament*
GOURNEY, *the King's keeper*
LIGHTBORNE, *an assassin*
THE KING'S CHAMPION
Lords, Attendants, Guards, Posts, Ladies-in-Waiting, Soldiers

3

[SCENE 1]

Enter GAVESTON *reading on a letter that was brought
him from the King*

GAVESTON

'My father is deceased; come, Gaveston,
And share the kingdom with thy dearest friend.'
Ah, words that make me surfeit with delight!
What greater bliss can hap to Gaveston,
Than live and be the favourite of a king?   5
Sweet prince, I come; these, these thy amorous lines
Might have enforced me to have swum from France,
And, like Leander, gasped upon the sand,
So thou wouldst smile and take me in thy arms.
The sight of London to my exiled eyes   10
Is as Elysium to a new-come soul;
Not that I love the city or the men,
But that it harbours him I hold so dear,
The King, upon whose bosom let me die,
And with the world be still at enmity.   15
What need the arctic people love starlight,
To whom the sun shines both by day and night?
Farewell, base stooping to the lordly peers;
My knee shall bow to none but to the King.
As for the multitude, that are but sparks   20
Raked up in embers of their poverty,

The traditional act-divisions are not adopted in this edition: see the Note on the Text.

3   *surfeit* indulge, gorge.
4   *hap to* happen to, befall.
7   *France* Gaveston had been exiled by order of Edward I to his home in Gascony.
8   *Leander* tragic lover in the classical story retold in Marlowe's narrative poem *Hero and Leander* (*c.* 1593). Leander fell in love with Hero and swam the Hellespont to Sestos every night in order to be with her. One night the light in the tower which guided Leander to the Sestos shore was blown out by a storm and he drowned. Hero committed suicide when Leander's body was washed up on the shore.
11   *Elysium* the islands of the blessed in classical mythology; equivalent to heaven.
14   *die* (i) swoon (ii) experience sexual orgasm.
20–1 *multitude . . . poverty* Gaveston, for whom the king is like the sun, disdains the common people as mere dull embers – they have to be raked even to show sparks of life. Merchant sees this metaphor as 'an extended play on the relationship between the sun as the principal light of the heavens and kingship and degree among men'.

Tanti! I'll fan first on the wind
That glanceth at my lips and flieth away.

Enter three POOR MEN

But how now, what are these?
POOR MEN
Such as desire your worship's service.   25
GAVESTON
What canst thou do?
FIRST POOR MAN
I can ride.
GAVESTON
But I have no horses. What art thou?
SECOND POOR MAN
A traveller.
GAVESTON
Let me see, thou wouldst do well to wait at my trencher and tell   30
me lies at dinner-time; and, as I like your discoursing, I'll have
you. And what art thou?
THIRD POOR MAN
A soldier, that hath served against the Scot.
GAVESTON
Why, there are hospitals for such as you;
I have no war, and therefore, sir, be gone.   35
THIRD POOR MAN
Farewell, and perish by a soldier's hand,
That wouldst reward them with an hospital.

22   *Tanti* 'So much for them!' (spoken with contempt).
22–3   *fan . . . flieth away* This image of blowing air to keep a fire's embers burning builds
        upon the imagery of lines 20–1; it also depicts Gaveston's impudent assumption
        that he can control the common people.
23   sd ed.; after line 24 in Q.
27   sp FIRST POOR MAN ed. (*1. poore.* Q).
29   sp SECOND POOR MAN ed. (*2. poore.* Q).
30   ed. (*Let . . . well / To . . . time, / And . . . you. / And . . . thou?* Q).
        trencher wooden plate.
31   *lies* travellers' tales. Cf. proverb, 'A traveller may lie with authority' (Tilley T 476).
        as if.
33   sp THIRD POOR MAN ed. (*3. poore.* Q).
        served . . . Scot England was troubled in the later years of Edward I's reign by a long
        war with Scotland, led by Robert Bruce.
34   *hospitals* charitable hospices for the needy.
36   sp THIRD POOR MAN ed. (*Sold.* Q).

GAVESTON [*Aside*]

    Ay, ay. These words of his move me as much

    As if a goose should play the porcupine,

    And dart her plumes, thinking to pierce my breast.   40

    But yet it is no pain to speak men fair;

    I'll flatter these, and make them live in hope.

    [*To them*] You know that I came lately out of France,

    And yet I have not viewed my lord the King;

    If I speed well, I'll entertain you all.   45

POOR MEN

    We thank your worship.

GAVESTON

    I have some business; leave me to myself.

POOR MEN

    We will wait here about the court.

                                         Exeunt

GAVESTON

    Do. These are not men for me;

    I must have wanton poets, pleasant wits,   50

    Musicians, that with touching of a string

    May draw the pliant King which way I please.

    Music and poetry is his delight;

    Therefore I'll have Italian masques by night,

    Sweet speeches, comedies, and pleasing shows;   55

    And in the day when he shall walk abroad,

    Like sylvan nymphs my pages shall be clad.

    My men like satyrs grazing on the lawns

---

40   *dart . . . plumes* The Elizabethans believed that porcupines would shoot their quills in self-defence.

45   *speed well* am successful.

       entertain take into service.

46, 48 sp POOR MEN ed. (*Omnes.* Q).

50   *wanton* lascivious.

       pleasant wits jocular, intelligent, and pleasing orators.

52   *pliant* malleable, readily influenced.

54   *masques* Courtly dramatic entertainments which originated in Italy and became popular in the English court during the late sixteenth and early seventeenth centuries. The earlier form of masque involved singing and dancing, in which the performers would be partially disguised by masks. The later development involved great costliness of scenes and costumes.

56   *abroad* outside, out of doors.

57   *sylvan nymphs* female wood spirits.

58   *satyrs* woodland demons which are part-human, part-goat, and are usually associated with Bacchus, the classical god of wine and revelry.

Shall with their goat-feet dance an antic hay;
Sometime a lovely boy in Dian's shape,   60
With hair that gilds the water as it glides,
Crownets of pearl about his naked arms,
And in his sportful hands an olive tree
To hide those parts which men delight to see,
Shall bathe him in a spring; and there hard by,   65
One like Actaeon peeping through the grove,
Shall by the angry goddess be transformed,
And running in the likeness of an hart,
By yelping hounds pulled down, and seem to die.
Such things as these best please his majesty.   70

> *Enter* [EDWARD] *the King,* LANCASTER, MORTIMER SENIOR,
> MORTIMER JUNIOR, EDMUND EARL OF KENT,
> GUY EARL OF WARWICK[, *and attendants*]

My lord! Here comes the King and the nobles
From the parliament; I'll stand aside.

EDWARD

Lancaster.

LANCASTER

My lord.

GAVESTON [*Aside*]

That Earl of Lancaster do I abhor.   75

EDWARD

Will you not grant me this? [*Aside*] In spite of them
I'll have my will, and these two Mortimers

---

59   *antic* grotesque.
      hay a country dance with a serpentine movement.
60   *Dian's shape* i.e. the appearance of Diana – in classical mythology, the moon goddess
      who was also associated with female chastity.
      gilds . . . glides i.e. covers the water with a golden colour. This image could also imply
      artifice: cf. Holland's translation of Pliny's *Naturalis Historia* (1601), 'I see that now
      adaies siluer only . . . is guilded by the means of this artificiall Quicksiluer.'
62   *Crownets* coronets.
63   *sportful* playful, sportive.
65   *hard by* close by, near.
66   *Actaeon* In classical mythology, the hunter who offended the goddess Diana by seeing
      her bathe naked. In her anger, she turned him into a stag, and he was later chased
      and killed by his own hounds. Cf. Ovid's *Metamorphoses*, III. 138 ff.
70   sd ed.: after line 72 in Q.
72   *stand aside* Gaveston withdraws to the side of the stage until line 138.

That cross me thus shall know I am displeased.
MORTIMER SENIOR
  If you love us, my lord, hate Gaveston.
GAVESTON [*Aside*]
  That villain Mortimer, I'll be his death.   80
MORTIMER JUNIOR
  Mine uncle here, this earl, and I myself
  Were sworn to your father at his death,
  That he should ne'er return into the realm;
  And know, my lord, ere I will break my oath,
  This sword of mine that should offend your foes,   85
  Shall sleep within the scabbard at thy need,
  And underneath thy banners march who will,
  For Mortimer will hang his armour up.
GAVESTON [*Aside*]
  Mort Dieu!
EDWARD
  Well Mortimer, I'll make thee rue these words.   90
  Beseems it thee to contradict thy King?
  Frownst thou thereat, aspiring Lancaster?
  The sword shall plane the furrows of thy brows
  And hew these knees that now are grown so stiff.
  I will have Gaveston; and you shall know   95
  What danger 'tis to stand against your King.
GAVESTON [*Aside*]
  Well done, Ned.
LANCASTER
  My lord, why do you thus incense your peers
  That naturally would love and honour you,
  But for that base and obscure Gaveston?   100
  Four earldoms have I besides Lancaster:

78   *cross* obstruct.
87   *banners* fringed flags which were carried as standards before an army.
89   *Mort Dieu!* A French oath meaning 'by God's death', reminding us of Gaveston's continental origins.
90   *rue* regret.
91   *Beseems it thee* i.e. is it fitting for you.
92   *thereat* at that.
97   *Ned* This diminutive emphasizes Gaveston's familiar relationship with the king.
99   *naturally* by nature, by birth (according to their social status).
100   *base* of low birth, poor stock.
       obscure lowly.

Derby, Salisbury, Lincoln, Leicester.
These will I sell to give my soldiers pay,
Ere Gaveston shall stay within the realm.
Therefore if he be come, expel him straight.   105

KENT

Barons and earls, your pride hath made me mute.
But now I'll speak, and to the proof I hope:
I do remember in my father's days,
Lord Percy of the North, being highly moved,
Braved Mowbery in presence of the King.   110
For which, had not his highness loved him well,
He should have lost his head, but with his look
The undaunted spirit of Percy was appeased,
And Mowbery and he were reconciled.
Yet dare you brave the King unto his face?   115
Brother, revenge it; and let these their heads
Preach upon poles for trespass of their tongues.

WARWICK

O, our heads!

EDWARD

Ay, yours; and therefore I would wish you grant.

WARWICK

Bridle thy anger, gentle Mortimer.   120

MORTIMER JUNIOR

I cannot, nor I will not; I must speak.
Cousin, our hands I hope shall fence our heads,
And strike off his that makes you threaten us.
Come uncle, let us leave the brainsick King,
And henceforth parley with our naked swords.   125

---

106   sp KENT ed. (*Edm.* Q; and throughout the text whenever '*Edm.*' is used).
107   *to the proof* irrefutably.
109   *moved* angry.
110   *Braved* challenged.
       Mowbery Mowbray (*Mowberie* Q; also at line 114).
117   *Preach . . . poles* After execution, traitors' severed heads were publicly displayed on
       poles as a warning to others.
119   *grant* assent.
122   *Cousin* a term used by a sovereign when formally addressing a nobleman. In this
       instance Mortimer Junior, being Edward's subject, uses the term presumptuously.
       fence shield.

MORTIMER SENIOR

Welshry hath men enough to save our heads.

WARWICK

All Warwickshire will love him for my sake.

LANCASTER

And northward Gaveston hath many friends.
Adieu my lord; and either change your mind,
Or look to see the throne where you should sit   130
To float in blood, and at thy wanton head
The glozing head of thy base minion thrown.

Exeunt NOBLES [*except* KENT]

EDWARD

I cannot brook these haughty menaces:
Am I a king and must be overruled?
Brother, display my ensigns in the field;   135
I'll bandy with the barons and the earls,
And either die or live with Gaveston.

GAVESTON

I can no longer keep me from my lord.   [*He steps forward*]

EDWARD

What, Gaveston! Welcome! Kiss not my hand;
Embrace me, Gaveston, as I do thee!   140
Why shouldst thou kneel; knowest thou not who I am?
Thy friend, thy self, another Gaveston!
Not Hylas was more mourned of Hercules
Than thou hast been of me since thy exile.

126   *Welshry* ed. (Wilshire Q) the Welsh populace. Roma Gill has pointed out that the
       policy of most editors to adopt the reading 'Wiltshire' is historically incorrect and
       may well have been a compositorial misreading for 'Welshrye'. Mortimer Senior was
       in fact Edward's Lieutenant and Justice of Wales, governing Wales from 1307 to 1321.
       See 'Mortimer's Men', *N&Q*, n.s. 27 (1980), 159.
128   spoken ironically, like the previous line: Lancaster means Gaveston has no friends at
       all in the north.
132   *glozing* flattering.
       minion A powerful man's favourite or homosexual lover; derived from the French
       mignon (= sweet), applied to the favourites of Henry III of France.
133   *brook* endure.   *menaces* threats.
135   *ensigns* military banners.   *in the field* in battle.
136   *bandy* give and take blows, as in a game of tennis.
141   ed. (Why . . . kneele, / Knowest . . . I am? Q).
143   *Hylas . . . Hercules* Hylas accompanied Hercules on the journey of the Argonauts.
       When they anchored at Mysia, Hylas was carried away by water-nymphs. In his grief,
       Hercules remained behind, searching for the lost boy while the Argonauts continued
       their journey.

GAVESTON

    And since I went from hence, no soul in hell   145
    Hath felt more torment than poor Gaveston.

EDWARD

    I know it. [*To* KENT] Brother, welcome home my friend.
    [*To* GAVESTON] Now let the treacherous Mortimers conspire.
    And that high-minded Earl of Lancaster.
    I have my wish, in that I joy thy sight,   150
    And sooner shall the sea o'erwhelm my land
    Than bear the ship that shall transport thee hence.
    I here create thee Lord High Chamberlain,
    Chief Secretary to the state and me,
    Earl of Cornwall, King and Lord of Man.   155

GAVESTON

    My lord, these titles far exceed my worth.

KENT

    Brother, the least of these may well suffice
    For one of greater birth than Gaveston.

EDWARD

    Cease, brother, for I cannot brook these words.
    [*To* GAVESTON] Thy worth, sweet friend, is far above my gifts,   160
    Therefore to equal it, receive my heart.
    If for these dignities thou be envied,
    I'll give thee more, for but to honour thee
    Is Edward pleased with kingly regiment.
    Fear'st thou thy person? Thou shalt have a guard.   165
    Wants thou gold? Go to my treasury.
    Wouldst thou be loved and feared? Receive my seal,
    Save or condemn, and in our name command
    What so thy mind affects or fancy likes.

GAVESTON

    It shall suffice me to enjoy your love,   170
    Which whiles I have, I think myself as great

---

149   *high-minded* arrogant.
150   *joy* enjoy.
155   *King . . . Man* Until 1829, the rulers of The Isle of Man were known as kings, possessing certain sovereign rights (Gill).
164   *regiment* rule.
167   *seal* A token of royal authority; in performance the seal is often in the form of a ring.
169   *affects* desires.
       fancy (i) caprice (ii) amorous inclination.

As Caesar riding in the Roman street,
With captive kings at his triumphant car.

Enter the BISHOP OF COVENTRY

EDWARD

Whither goes my lord of Coventry so fast?

BISHOP OF COVENTRY

To celebrate your father's exequies.   175
But is that wicked Gaveston returned?

EDWARD

Ay, priest, and lives to be revenged on thee
That wert the only cause of his exile.

GAVESTON

'Tis true, and but for reverence of these robes
Thou shouldst not plod one foot beyond this place.   180

BISHOP OF COVENTRY

I did no more than I was bound to do;
And Gaveston, unless thou be reclaimed,
As then I did incense the parliament,
So will I now, and thou shalt back to France.

GAVESTON

Saving your reverence, you must pardon me.   185

EDWARD

Throw off his golden mitre, rend his stole,
And in the channel christen him anew.

[*Assaults* COVENTRY]

KENT

Ah brother, lay not violent hands on him,
For he'll complain unto the See of Rome.

172–3   *Caesar . . . kings* a popular image of conquest. Cf. George Peele's *Edward I*: 'Not
          Caesar leading through the streetes of Rome, / The captive kings of conquered
          nations, / Was in his princely triumphes honoured more' (i. 91–3).
172   *car* chariot.
175   sp *BISHOP OF COVENTRY* ed. (*Bish.* Q; also at ll. 181, 198, and 200).
          exequies funeral rites.
182   *reclaimed* reformed, subdued.
183   *incense* incite.
185   *Saving your reverence* a sarcastic rendering of a proverbial expression which was
          usually said apologetically (Tilley R 93).
186   *golden mitre* head-dress which was a symbol of episcopal office; rarely worn in the
          Anglican Church after the Reformation.
          rend tear.   *stole* ecclesiastical vestment.
187   *channel* gutter. For the exact nature of the violence done to the Bishop, cf. 2.35–6.
189   *See of Rome* i.e. the Pope.

13

GAVESTON

    Let him complain unto the See of Hell;   190

    I'll be revenged on him for my exile.

EDWARD

    No, spare his life, but seize upon his goods.

    Be thou lord bishop, and receive his rents.

    And make him serve thee as thy chaplain.

    I give him thee; here, use him as thou wilt.   195

GAVESTON

    He shall to prison, and there die in bolts.

EDWARD

    Ay, to the Tower, the Fleet, or where thou wilt.

BISHOP OF COVENTRY

    For this offence be thou accurst of God.

EDWARD

    Who's there?

[*Enter* GUARDS]

    Convey this priest to the Tower.

BISHOP OF COVENTRY

    True, true!   200

[*Exit* BISHOP *and* GUARDS]

EDWARD

    But in the meantime Gaveston, away,

    And take possession of his house and goods.

    Come, follow me, and thou shalt have my guard

    To see it done and bring thee safe again.

GAVESTON

    What should a priest do with so fair a house?   205

    A prison may beseem his holiness.

[*Exeunt*]

192   *goods* property, possessions.

193   *rents* (i) revenues, income (ii) taxes levied by the Church.

196   *bolts* fetters.

197   *the Fleet* in Marlowe's time, a prison which stood between the River Thames and Ludgate Hill.

198   *accurst* doomed to damnation.

199   *Convey* conduct, escort.

203   *guard* (i) body of soldiers (ii) guardianship, safe conduct.

205   *fair* fine, beautiful.

206   *beseem* be fitting, more appropriate (because of the meagre conditions which are commonly associated with a priest's cell).

[SCENE 2]

· *Enter both the* MORTIMERS [*on one side*],
WARWICK, *and* LANCASTER [*on the other*]

WARWICK

'Tis true, the Bishop is in the Tower,
And goods and body given to Gaveston.

LANCASTER

What, will they tyrannize upon the Church?
Ah, wicked King! Accursèd Gaveston!
This ground which is corrupted with their steps   5
Shall be their timeless sepulchre, or mine.

MORTIMER JUNIOR

Well, let that peevish Frenchman guard him sure;
Unless his breast be sword-proof he shall die.

MORTIMER SENIOR

How now, why droops the Earl of Lancaster?

MORTIMER JUNIOR

Wherefore is Guy of Warwick discontent?   10

LANCASTER

That villain Gaveston is made an earl.

MORTIMER SENIOR

An earl!

WARWICK

Ay, and besides, Lord Chamberlain of the realm,
And Secretary too, and Lord of Man.

MORTIMER SENIOR

We may not, nor we will not suffer this.   15

---

0   sd Characters usually entered the Elizabethan stage through two or more doors set
    into the rear wall. Entry through different doors (as editorially indicated here)
    signified that they had come from different directions.
3   *tyrannize* Edward is acting tyrannically in that, by imprisoning the Bishop, he is
    usurping the spiritual power of the Church.
6   *timeless* (i) eternal (ii) untimely.
    sepulchre tomb, grave.
7   *peevish* foolish.
    him himself.
    sure securely.
11 *villain* (i) rascal, scoundrel (ii) serf, bondman (deriving from 'villein', one of low birth).
15 *suffer* tolerate.

MORTIMER JUNIOR

    Why post we not from hence to levy men?

LANCASTER

    'My Lord of Cornwall' now at every word;

    And happy is the man whom he vouchsafes

    For vailing of his bonnet one good look.

    Thus, arm in arm, the King and he doth march –   20

    Nay more, the guard upon his lordship waits,

    And all the court begins to flatter him.

WARWICK

    Thus leaning on the shoulder of the King,

    He nods, and scorns, and smiles at those that pass.

MORTIMER SENIOR

    Doth no man take exceptions at the slave?   25

LANCASTER

    All stomach him, but none dare speak a word.

MORTIMER JUNIOR

    Ah, that bewrays their baseness, Lancaster.

    Were all the earls and barons of my mind,

    We'll hale him from the bosom of the King,

    And at the court gate hang the peasant up,   30

    Who, swoll'n with venom of ambitious pride,

    Will be the ruin of the realm and us.

Enter the BISHOP OF CANTERBURY [, *talking*
to an ATTENDANT]

WARWICK

    Here comes my lord of Canterbury's grace.

LANCASTER

    His countenance bewrays he is displeased.

BISHOP OF CANTERBURY [*To* ATTENDANT]

    First were his sacred garments rent and torn,   35

16   *post* i.e. travel with speed.   *levy men* assemble soldiers.

19   *vailing* doffing.

24   s*corns* mocks.

26   *stomach* resent.

27   *bewrays* reveals.

29   *hale* draw, drag.

31   *Who . . . pride* Cf. *Dr Faustus*, 'Till, swoll'n with cunning of a self-conceit' (A-Text,
      Prologue, 20).

33   *grace* i.e. his grace (formal term of address).

34   *countenance* face, demeanour.   *bewrays* betrays.

35   sp BISHOP OF CANTERBURY ed. (*Bish.* Q; also at ll. 40, 44, 61, 68, and 75).

Then laid they violent hands upon him next,
Himself imprisoned and his goods asseized;
This certify the Pope. Away, take horse.

[Exit ATTENDANT]

LANCASTER

My lord, will you take arms against the King?

BISHOP OF CANTERBURY

What need I? God himself is up in arms   40
When violence is offered to the Church.

MORTIMER JUNIOR

Then will you join with us that be his peers
To banish or behead that Gaveston?

BISHOP OF CANTERBURY

What else, my lords? For it concerns me near;
The bishopric of Coventry is his.   45

Enter [ISABELLA] *the Queen*

MORTIMER JUNIOR

Madam, whither walks your majesty so fast?

ISABELLA

Unto the forest, gentle Mortimer,
To live in grief and baleful discontent;
For now my lord the King regards me not,
But dotes upon the love of Gaveston.   50
He claps his cheeks and hangs about his neck,
Smiles in his face and whispers in his ears;
And when I come he frowns, as who should say,
'Go whither thou wilt, seeing I have Gaveston.'

MORTIMER SENIOR

Is it not strange that he is thus bewitched?   55

---

37   *asseized* seized.
38   *certify* inform (with certainty).
44   *near* (i) deeply (ii) personally (in that, by becoming a bishop, Gaveston becomes
      a matter of direct concern to Canterbury).
45   *bishopric* diocese.
47   sp ISABELLA ed. (*Que.* Q; and throughout the play text).
      forest wastelands; a metaphorical expression which describes Isabella's feelings of
      isolation.
      gentle kind.
48   *baleful* wretched.
49   *regards* considers.
51   *claps* slaps affectionately.

17

MORTIMER JUNIOR

    Madam, return unto the court again.

    That sly inveigling Frenchman we'll exile,

    Or lose our lives; and yet, ere that day come,

    The King shall lose his crown, for we have power

    And courage too, to be revenged at full.   60

BISHOP OF CANTERBURY

    But yet lift not your swords against the King.

LANCASTER

    No, but we'll lift Gaveston from hence.

WARWICK

    And war must be the means, or he'll stay still.

ISABELLA

    Then let him stay; for rather than my lord

    Shall be oppressed by civil mutinies,   65

    I will endure a melancholy life,

    And let him frolic with his minion.

BISHOP OF CANTERBURY

    My lords, to ease all this but hear me speak.

    We and the rest that are his councillors

    Will meet and with a general consent   70

    Confirm his banishment with our hands and seals.

LANCASTER

    What we confirm the King will frustrate.

MORTIMER JUNIOR

    Then may we lawfully revolt from him.

WARWICK

    But say, my lord, where shall this meeting be?

BISHOP OF CANTERBURY

    At the New Temple.   75

57   *inveigling* deceiving.

58   *ere* before.

62   *lift* (i) steal (ii) raise (by hanging).

63   *still* always.

67   *frolic* make merry (with overtones of sexual promiscuity).

68   *but* only.

72   *frustrate* annul, defeat.

75   *New Temple* a building established and used by the Knights Templar until their suppression in 1308.

MORTIMER JUNIOR
Content.
BISHOP OF CANTERBURY
And in the meantime I'll entreat you all
To cross to Lambeth, and there stay with me.
LANCASTER
Come then, let's away.
MORTIMER JUNIOR
Madam, farewell.   80
ISABELLA
Farewell, sweet Mortimer; and for my sake.
Forbear to levy arms against the King.
MORTIMER JUNIOR
Ay, if words will serve; if not, I must.

[*Exeunt*]

[SCENE 3]

Enter GAVESTON *and the* EARL OF KENT

GAVESTON
Edmund, the mighty prince of Lancaster,
That hath more earldoms than an ass can bear.
And both the Mortimers, two goodly men,
With Guy of Warwick, that redoubted knight,
Are gone towards Lambeth; there let them remain.   5

Exeunt

77   sp BISHOP OF CANTERBURY ed. (not in Q); (*Mor. iu.* Content. And . . . all, / To crosse
      . . . me. Q).
78   *Lambeth* Lambeth Palace, the official residence of the Archbishop of Canterbury.

1   Gaveston addresses Kent familiarly by his personal name.
4   *redoubted* feared.

[SCENE 4]

Enter NOBLES [LANCASTER, WARWICK, PEMBROKE,
MORTIMER SENIOR, MORTIMER JUNIOR, *and the*
BISHOP OF CANTERBURY, *with attendants*]

LANCASTER

Here is the form of Gaveston's exile;

May it please your lordship to subscribe your name.

BISHOP OF CANTERBURY

Give me the paper.

LANCASTER

Quick, quick, my lord; I long to write my name.

WARWICK

But I long more to see him banished hence.   5

MORTIMER JUNIOR

The name of Mortimer shall fright the King,

Unless he be declined from that base peasant.

Enter [EDWARD] *the King and* GAVESTON[, *with* KENT].
[EDWARD *assumes the throne, with* GAVESTON *at his side*]

EDWARD

What, are you moved that Gaveston sits here?

It is our pleasure; we will have it so.

LANCASTER

Your grace doth well to place him by your side,   10

For nowhere else the new Earl is so safe.

MORTIMER SENIOR

What man of noble birth can brook this sight?

---

 0 sd Q uses the terms 'nobles' and 'barons' indifferently to refer to the rebel lords.
 1 *form* document.
 3 sp BISHOP OF CANTERBURY ed. (*Bish* Q; and throughout the scene).
 7 *declined* turned aside.
 8 *sits here* 'Gaveston's seat beside the king (where the queen would normally sit) is
    both emblematic and shocking; it signifies that Edward has made his lover politically
    equal with himself' (Forker).
 9 *pleasure* will.
11 *new Earl* The emphasis on 'new' reiterates the nobles' annoyance that such an
    'upstart' has acquired, not inherited, his aristocratic status.

Quam male conveniunt!
See what a scornful look the peasant casts.

PEMBROKE

Can kingly lions fawn on creeping ants?   15

WARWICK

Ignoble vassal, that like Phaëthon
Aspir'st unto the guidance of the sun.

MORTIMER JUNIOR

Their downfall is at hand, their forces down;
We will not thus be faced and over-peered.

EDWARD

Lay hands on that traitor Mortimer!   20

MORTIMER SENIOR

Lay hands on that traitor Gaveston!

[*The* NOBLES *draw swords*]

KENT

Is this the duty that you owe your King?

WARWICK

We know our duties; let him know his peers.

[*The* NOBLES *seize* GAVESTON]

EDWARD

Whither will you bear him? Stay, or ye shall die.

MORTIMER SENIOR

We are no traitors, therefore threaten not.   25

GAVESTON

No, threaten not, my lord, but pay them home.
Were I a king –

MORTIMER JUNIOR

Thou villain, wherefore talks thou of a king.

13 *Quam male conveniunt!* How badly they go together (i.e. match, suit one another)!
    Derived from Ovid's *Metamorphoses*, II. 846–7.
14 *scornful* derisive, contemptuous.
16 *Ignoble* of low birth.
    vassal slave.
    Phaëthon in classical mythology, the son of Phoebus Apollo (the sun god), who
    ignored warnings not to drive his father's chariot, lost control, and caused
    devastation on earth before the chariot was destroyed by Jupiter. In the sixteenth
    century, the story was commonly used as an emblem of the fall of overweening
    ambition. Cf. Ovid's *Metamorphoses*, I. 755 ff.
19 *faced* bullied.
    over-peered looked down upon (with pun on 'peer' = nobleman).
24 *bear* conduct, take.
26 *pay them home* chastise them.

That hardly art a gentleman by birth?

EDWARD

Were he a peasant, being my minion,   30
I'll make the proudest of you stoop to him.

LANCASTER

My lord, you may not thus disparage us.
Away, I say, with hateful Gaveston.

MORTIMER SENIOR

And with the Earl of Kent that favours him.

                              [*Exeunt* GAVESTON *and* KENT *guarded*]

EDWARD

Nay, then lay violent hands upon your King.   35
Here, Mortimer, sit thou in Edward's throne;
Warwick and Lancaster, wear you my crown.
Was ever king thus overruled as I?

LANCASTER

Learn then to rule us better and the realm.

MORTIMER JUNIOR

What we have done, our heart-blood shall maintain.   40

WARWICK

Think you that we can brook this upstart pride?

EDWARD

Anger and wrathful fury stops my speech.

BISHOP OF CANTERBURY

Why are you moved? Be patient, my lord.
And see what we your councillors have done.

        [*He presents the document of* GAVESTON*'s exile to* EDWARD]

MORTIMER JUNIOR

My lords, now let us all be resolute,   45
And either have our wills or lose our lives.

EDWARD

Meet you for this, proud overdaring peers?
Ere my sweet Gaveston shall part from me,
This isle shall fleet upon the ocean
And wander to the unfrequented Inde.   50

---

32   *disparage* vilify; 'originally meant to degrade by marrying to one of inferior rank'
       (Charlton and Waller).
47   *overdaring* imprudent, foolhardy.
49   *fleet* float.
50   *Inde* East Indies.

BISHOP OF CANTERBURY
    You know that I am legate to the Pope;
    On your allegiance to the See of Rome,
    Subscribe as we have done to his exile.
MORTIMER JUNIOR
    Curse him if he refuse, and then may we
    Depose him and elect another king.   55
EDWARD
    Ay, there it goes, but yet I will not yield.
    Curse me. Depose me. Do the worst you can.
LANCASTER
    Then linger not, my lord, but do it straight.
BISHOP OF CANTERBURY
    Remember how the Bishop was abused;
    Either banish him that was the cause thereof,   60
    Or I will presently discharge these lords
    Of duty and allegiance due to thee.
EDWARD
    It boots me not to threat; I must speak fair,
    The legate of the Pope will be obeyed.
    My lord, you shall be Chancellor of the realm;   65
    Thou Lancaster, High Admiral of our fleet.
    Young Mortimer and his uncle shall be earls,
    And you, Lord Warwick, President of the North,
    [*To* PEMBROKE] And thou of Wales. If this content you not,
    Make several kingdoms of this monarchy,   70
    And share it equally amongst you all,
    So I may have some nook or corner left
    To frolic with my dearest Gaveston.
BISHOP OF CANTERBURY
    Nothing shall alter us; we are resolved.
LANCASTER
    Come, come, subscribe.   75

---

51   *legate* deputy, representative.
54   *Curse* excommunicate.
59   *abused* insulted, ill-used (violently).
61–2 The subjects of an excommunicated monarch were absolved of their duty of
       obedience; Elizabeth I had been excommunicated by Pope Pius V in 1570.
63   *boots* avails.
68   *President of the North* Gill cites John Cowell's *The Interpreter* (1607): 'President . . .
       is used in Common law for the kings Lieutenant in any Province or function; as
       President of Wales, of York, of Barwick.'

MORTIMER JUNIOR

Why should you love him whom the world hates so?

EDWARD

Because he loves me more than all the world.

Ah, none but rude and savage-minded men

Would seek the ruin of my Gaveston;

You that be noble born should pity him.   80

WARWICK

You that are princely born should shake him off.

For shame subscribe, and let the lown depart.

MORTIMER SENIOR

Urge him, my lord.

BISHOP OF CANTERBURY

Are you content to banish him the realm?

EDWARD

I see I must, and therefore am content;   85

Instead of ink, I'll write it with my tears.

　　　　　　　　　　　　　　　　[*He signs the document*]

MORTIMER JUNIOR

The King is love-sick for his minion.

EDWARD

'Tis done, and now accursed hand fall off.

LANCASTER

Give it me; I'll have it published in the streets.

MORTIMER JUNIOR

I'll see him presently dispatched away.   90

BISHOP OF CANTERBURY

Now is my heart at ease.

WARWICK　　　　　　　　　　　　And so is mine.

PEMBROKE

This will be good news to the common sort.

MORTIMER SENIOR

Be it or no, he shall not linger here.

　　　　　　　Exeunt NOBLES[, *the* BISHOP OF CANTERBURY,

　　　　　　　　　　　　　　　　　　　and attendants]

78　　*rude* uncivilized.
82　　*lown* peasant.
89　　*published* proclaimed.
90　　*presently* immediately.
92　　*common sort* i.e. the common people.

24

EDWARD

How fast they run to banish him I love;
They would not stir, were it to do me good.   95
Why should a king be subject to a priest?
Proud Rome, that hatchest such imperial grooms,
For these thy superstitious taper-lights,
Wherewith thy antichristian churches blaze,
I'll fire thy crazèd buildings and enforce   100
The papal towers to kiss the lowly ground,
With slaughtered priests make Tiber's channel swell,
And banks raised higher with their sepulchres.
As for the peers that back the clergy thus,
If I be King, not one of them shall live.   105

Enter GAVESTON

GAVESTON

My lord, I hear it whispered everywhere
That I am banished and must fly the land.

EDWARD

'Tis true, sweet Gaveston. O were it false!
The legate of the Pope will have it so,
And thou must hence, or I shall be deposed.   110
But I will reign to be revenged of them,
And therefore, sweet friend, take it patiently.
Live where thou wilt – I'll send thee gold enough.
And long thou shalt not stay, or if thou dost,
I'll come to thee; my love shall ne'er decline.   115

GAVESTON

Is all my hope turned to this hell of grief?

EDWARD

Rend not my heart with thy too-piercing words.
Thou from this land, I from my self am banished.

GAVESTON

To go from hence grieves not poor Gaveston,

95   *stir* act.
97   *imperial* imperious.
      grooms servants.
98   *taper-lights* candles for devotional and penitential use.
100   *crazèd* shattered, unsound. Cf. *Massacre at Paris*, 'I'll fire his crazed buildings, and
      incense / The papal towers to kiss the holy earth' (xxiv. 62–3).
102   *make* ed. (may Q).
      Tiber's channel the River Tiber in Rome.

25

But to forsake you, in whose gracious looks   120
The blessedness of Gaveston remains,
For nowhere else seeks he felicity.

EDWARD

And only this torments my wretched soul,
That whether I will or no, thou must depart.
Be Governor of Ireland in my stead,   125
And there abide till fortune call thee home.
Here, take my picture, and let me wear thine.

                              [*They exchange miniatures*]

O might I keep thee here, as I do this,
Happy were I, but now most miserable.

GAVESTON

'Tis something to be pitied of a king.   130

EDWARD

Thou shalt not hence; I'll hide thee, Gaveston.

GAVESTON

I shall be found, and then 'twill grieve me more.

EDWARD

Kind words and mutual talk makes our grief greater.
Therefore, with dumb embracement, let us part –
Stay, Gaveston, I cannot leave thee thus.   135

GAVESTON

For every look my lord drops down a tear;
Seeing I must go, do not renew my sorrow.

EDWARD

The time is little that thou hast to stay,
And therefore give me leave to look my fill.
But come, sweet friend, I'll bear thee on thy way.   140

GAVESTON

The peers will frown.

EDWARD

I pass not for their anger; come, let's go.
O that we might as well return as go.

121   *blessedness* superlative happiness.
131   *hence* i.e. go.
134   *dumb* silent.
140   *bear* accompany.
142   *pass* care.

Enter EDMUND [EARL OF KENT] *and Queen* ISABELLA

ISABELLA

Whither goes my lord?

EDWARD

Fawn not on me, French strumpet; get thee gone. 145

ISABELLA

On whom but on my husband should I fawn?

GAVESTON

On Mortimer, with whom, ungentle Queen –

I say no more; judge you the rest, my lord.

ISABELLA

In saying this, thou wrongst me, Gaveston.

Is't not enough that thou corrupts my lord, 150

And art a bawd to his affections,

But thou must call mine honour thus in question?

GAVESTON

I mean not so; your grace must pardon me.

EDWARD

Thou art too familiar with that Mortimer,

And by thy means is Gaveston exiled; 155

But I would wish thee reconcile the lords,

Or thou shalt ne'er be reconciled to me.

ISABELLA

Your highness knows it lies not in my power.

EDWARD

Away then, touch me not; come Gaveston.

143   sd ed. (*Enter Edmund and Queen Isabell.* Q) Kent has no lines, and there is a problem
        in finding a suitable point for him to exit. Other editors have reasoned that his
        presence is superfluous, detracting from the dramatic tension between the three
        lovers, and have deleted him from the stage direction. However, his presence as a
        silent witness to Edward's behaviour contributes a political dimension to an other-
        wise exclusively personal sequence, and helps to clarify the character's confused
        loyalties and subsequent changing allegiances.

145   *strumpet* sexually loose woman, prostitute.

147   Gaveston makes the first insinuation of adultery between Isabella and Mortimer
        Junior.

149   To accuse a woman unjustly of sexual misconduct was a grave misdemeanour in
        Elizabethan England.

150   *my lord* implying 'husband' as well as 'sovereign'.

151   *bawd* procurer, pander.
        affections (i) desires, inclinations (ii) passions (with sexual overtones).

ISABELLA

Villain, 'tis thou that robb'st me of my lord.   160

GAVESTON

Madam, 'tis you that rob me of my lord.

EDWARD

Speak not unto her; let her droop and pine.

ISABELLA

Wherein, my lord, have I deserved these words?
Witness the tears that Isabella sheds,
Witness this heart, that sighing for thee breaks,   165
How dear my lord is to poor Isabel.

EDWARD

And witness heaven how dear thou art to me.
There weep; for till my Gaveston be repealed,
Assure thyself thou com'st not in my sight.

> *Exeunt* EDWARD *and* GAVESTON.
> [*Exit* KENT *at the other door*]

ISABELLA

O miserable and distressèd Queen!   170
Would when I left sweet France and was embarked,
That charming Circe, walking on the waves,
Had changed my shape, or at the marriage-day
The cup of Hymen had been full of poison,
Or with those arms that twined about my neck   175
I had been stifled, and not lived to see
The King my lord thus to abandon me.
Like frantic Juno will I fill the earth
With ghastly murmur of my sighs and cries,
For never doted Jove on Ganymede   180

163   *Wherein* in what.
167   *witness . . . to me At* this point many productions have Edward and Gaveston
          embrace or kiss as lovers.
168   *repealed* recalled from exile.
169   sd *the other door* cf. 2.0 sd n.
172   *Circe* witch who turned Odysseus' men into pigs. See Homer's *Odyssey*, X and Ovid's
          Metamorphoses, XIV. 48ff.
174   *Hymen* god of marriage.
175   *those arms* i.e. Edward's arms (embracing Isabella).
178–80 *frantic Juno . . . Ganymede* In classical mythology, Juno became jealous when her
          husband Jove chose Ganymede to be his cup-bearer on account of his beauty.
          Marlowe dramatizes this homoerotic liaison in *Dido, Queen of Carthage*, I.i. See also
          Ovid's *Metamorphoses*, X. 155–61.
179   *murmur* (i) rumour (ii) expression of discontent.

So much as he on cursèd Gaveston.
But that will more exasperate his wrath;
I must entreat him, I must speak him fair,
And be a means to call home Gaveston.
And yet he'll ever dote on Gaveston,   185
And so am I forever miserable.

Enter the NOBLES [LANCASTER, WARWICK,
PEMBROKE, MORTIMER SENIOR, *and* MORTIMER JUNIOR]
to [ISABELLA] *the Queen*

LANCASTER
Look where the sister of the King of France
Sits wringing of her hands and beats her breast.

WARWICK
The King, I fear, hath ill entreated her.

PEMBROKE
Hard is the heart that injures such a saint.   190

MORTIMER JUNIOR
I know 'tis long of Gaveston she weeps.

MORTIMER SENIOR
Why? He is gone.

MORTIMER JUNIOR
Madam, how fares your grace?

ISABELLA
Ah, Mortimer! Now breaks the King's hate forth,
And he confesseth that he loves me not.

MORTIMER JUNIOR
Cry quittance, madam, then; and love not him.   195

ISABELLA
No, rather will I die a thousand deaths.
And yet I love in vain; he'll ne'er love me.

LANCASTER
Fear ye not, madam; now his minion's gone,
His wanton humour will be quickly left.

182   *exasperate* irritate, aggravate.
183   *entreat* negotiate with.   *fair* with kindness, courteously.
185   *ever* always.
189   *entreated* treated.
191   *long of* on account of.
195   *Cry quittance* (i) retaliate (ii) renounce the marriage bond (legal terminology).
199   *humour* temperament, disposition. The Elizabethans believed that humours or
       bodily fluids (phlegm, blood, choler, melancholy) were responsible for the state of
       a person's mind and body.

ISABELLA

O never, Lancaster! I am enjoined   200
To sue unto you all for his repeal.
This wills my lord, and this must I perform
Or else be banished from his highness' presence.

LANCASTER

For his repeal! Madam, he comes not back
Unless the sea cast up his shipwrack body.   205

WARWICK

And to behold so sweet a sight as that
There's none here but would run his horse to death.

MORTIMER JUNIOR

But madam, would you have us call him home?

ISABELLA

Ay, Mortimer, for till he be restored,
The angry King hath banished me the court;   210
And therefore, as thou lovest and tend'rest me,
Be thou my advocate unto these peers.

MORTIMER JUNIOR

What, would ye have me plead for Gaveston?

MORTIMER SENIOR

Plead for him he that will, I am resolved.

LANCASTER

And so am I; my lord, dissuade the Queen.   215

ISABELLA

O Lancaster, let him dissuade the King,
For 'tis against my will he should return.

WARWICK

Then speak not for him; let the peasant go.

ISABELLA

'Tis for myself I speak, and not for him.

PEMBROKE

No speaking will prevail, and therefore cease.   220

MORTIMER JUNIOR

Fair Queen, forbear to angle for the fish
Which, being caught, strikes him that takes it dead –

200   *enjoined* obliged, bound by oath.
201   *sue* beg.
205   *cast* throw up, vomit.
       shipwrack shipwrecked.
211   *tend'rest* care for.

30

I mean that vile torpedo, Gaveston,
That now, I hope, floats on the Irish seas.

ISABELLA

Sweet Mortimer, sit down by me a while,   225
And I will tell thee reasons of such weight
As thou wilt soon subscribe to his repeal.

MORTIMER JUNIOR

It is impossible; but speak your mind.

ISABELLA

Then thus – but none shall hear it but ourselves.
                [ISABELLA *and* MORTIMER JUNIOR *talk apart*]

LANCASTER

My lords, albeit the Queen win Mortimer,   230
Will you be resolute and hold with me?

MORTIMER SENIOR

Not I, against my nephew.

PEMBROKE

Fear not, the Queen's words cannot alter him.

WARWICK

No? Do but mark how earnestly she pleads.

LANCASTER

And see how coldly his looks make denial.   235

WARWICK

She smiles! Now, for my life, his mind is changed.

LANCASTER

I'll rather lose his friendship, I, than grant.

MORTIMER JUNIOR [*Returning to them*]

Well, of necessity, it must be so.
My lords, that I abhor base Gaveston
I hope your honours make no question;   240
And therefore, though I plead for his repeal,
'Tis not for his sake, but for our avail –
Nay, for the realm's behoof and for the King's.

223   *torpedo* electric ray, cramp-fish.
224   *floats* sails.
226   *weight* importance.
234   *mark* observe.
235   *make denial* refuse (to be persuaded).
237   *grant* assent, agree (to Isabella's will).
242   *avail* advantage.
243   *behoof* benefit.

LANCASTER

    Fie Mortimer, dishonour not thyself!

    Can this be true, 'twas good to banish him?   245

    And is this true, to call him home again?

    Such reasons make white black and dark night day.

MORTIMER JUNIOR

    My lord of Lancaster, mark the respect.

LANCASTER

    In no respect can contraries be true.

ISABELLA

    Yet, good my lord, hear what he can allege.   250

WARWICK

    All that he speaks is nothing; we are resolved.

MORTIMER JUNIOR

    Do you not wish that Gaveston were dead?

PEMBROKE

    I would he were.

MORTIMER JUNIOR

    Why then, my lord, give me but leave to speak.

MORTIMER SENIOR

    But nephew, do not play the sophister.   255

MORTIMER JUNIOR

    This which I urge is of a burning zeal

    To mend the King and do our country good.

    Know you not Gaveston hath store of gold,

    Which may in Ireland purchase him such friends

    As he will front the mightiest of us all?   260

    And whereas he shall live and be beloved,

    'Tis hard for us to work his overthrow.

WARWICK

    Mark you but that, my lord of Lancaster.

MORTIMER JUNIOR

    But were he here, detested as he is,

247   *Such reasons . . . day* proverbial (Tilley B 440).
248   *respect* consideration, special circumstances.
251   *nothing* i.e. irrelevant.
254   *give me . . . leave* allow me.
255   *sophister* philosopher who uses fallacious arguments.
257   *mend* reform.
260   *front* confront.
261   *whereas* while.
262   *work* effect, bring about.

How easily might some base slave be suborned   265
To greet his lordship with a poniard,
And none so much as blame the murderer,
But rather praise him for that brave attempt,
And in the chronicle, enrol his name
For purging of the realm of such a plague.   270

PEMBROKE
He saith true.

LANCASTER
Ay, but how chance this was not done before?

MORTIMER JUNIOR
Because, my lords, it was not thought upon.
Nay more, when he shall know it lies in us
To banish him, and then to call him home,   275
'Twill make him vail the topflag of his pride
And fear to offend the meanest nobleman.

MORTIMER SENIOR
But how if he do not, nephew?

MORTIMER JUNIOR
Then may we with some colour rise in arms,
For howsoever we have borne it out,   280
'Tis treason to be up against the King.
So shall we have the people of our side,
Which, for his father's sake, lean to the King
But cannot brook a night-grown mushroom –
Such a one as my lord of Cornwall is –   285
Should bear us down of the nobility.
And when the commons and the nobles join,
'Tis not the King can buckler Gaveston;

265   *suborned* bribed.
266   *poniard* dagger.
268   *brave* excellent, worthy
       attempt attack, assault.
276   *vail* lower.
277   *meanest* i.e. of the lowest rank.
279   *colour* pretext.
280   *howsoever . . . borne it out* however much we have endured.
282   *of* on.
284   *mushroom* ed. (mushrump Q1–4) Mushrooms grow overnight; hence a metaphor
       for an upstart, someone who has suddenly acquired reputation and influence.
       Proverbial (Tilley M 1319).
286   i.e. should overwhelm us, members of the nobility.
288   *buckler* shield.

We'll pull him from the strongest hold he hath.
My lords, if to perform this I be slack,   290
Think me as base a groom as Gaveston.

LANCASTER
On that condition Lancaster will grant.

PEMBROKE
And so will Pembroke.

WARWICK
And I.

MORTIMER SENIOR
And I.   295

MORTIMER JUNIOR
In this I count me highly gratified,
And Mortimer will rest at your command.

ISABELLA
And when this favour Isabel forgets,
Then let her live abandoned and forlorn.

Enter KING EDWARD *mourning*[, *with* BEAUMONT,
the CLERK OF THE CROWN, *and attendants*]

But see, in happy time, my lord the King,   300
Having brought the Earl of Cornwall on his way,
Is new returned. This news will glad him much,
Yet not so much as me; I love him more
Than he can Gaveston. Would he loved me
But half so much, then were I treble blessed.   305

EDWARD
He's gone, and for his absence thus I mourn.
Did never sorrow go so near my heart
As doth the want of my sweet Gaveston;
And could my crown's revenue bring him back,
I would freely give it to his enemies   310
And think I gained, having bought so dear a friend.

ISABELLA
Hark how he harps upon his minion.

EDWARD
My heart is as an anvil unto sorrow,

289   *hold* stronghold, castle.
293   sp PEMBROKE ed. (*War.* Q); (one line in Q And so will *Pembrooke* and *I*).
296   *gratified* pleased, content.
299   sd ed.; after line 303 in Q.

34

Which beats upon it like the Cyclops' hammers,
And with the noise turns up my giddy brain   315
And makes me frantic for my Gaveston.
Ah, had some bloodless Fury rose from hell,
And with kingly sceptre struck me dead,
When I was forced to leave my Gaveston.

LANCASTER

Diablo! What passions call you these?   320

ISABELLA

My gracious lord, I come to bring you news.

EDWARD

That you have parlied with your Mortimer.

ISABELLA

That Gaveston, my lord, shall be repealed.

EDWARD

Repealed? The news is too sweet to be true.

ISABELLA

But will you love me if you find it so?   325

EDWARD

If it be so, what will not Edward do?

ISABELLA

For Gaveston, but not for Isabel.

EDWARD

For thee, fair Queen, if thou lov'st Gaveston;
I'll hang a golden tongue about thy neck,
Seeing thou hast pleaded with so good success.   330
                                    [*He embraces her*]

ISABELLA

No other jewels hang about my neck
Than these, my lord; nor let me have more wealth

314   *Cyclops* in classical mythology, one-eyed giants employed to forge thunderbolts for
       Jupiter.
315   *up* i.e. upside down.
317   *Fury* In classical mythology, the Furies punished wrongdoers, and lived in Tartarus
       (a part of the underworld).
320   *Diabolo!* (Spanish) the devil!
       passions (i) lamentations, passionate speeches (ii) intense expressions of love.
324   *The news ... true* proverbial (Tilley N 156).
329   *golden tongue* an item of jewellery. Charlton and Waller cite *The Account of the Lord
       High Treasurer of Scotland (1488–92)*, 'A grete serpent toung set with gold, perle and
       precious stanes'.
332   *Than these* i.e. Edward's arms (embracing her).

Than I may fetch from this rich treasury.
O how a kiss revives poor Isabel.

EDWARD

Once more receive my hand, and let this be   335
A second marriage 'twixt thyself and me.

ISABELLA

And may it prove more happy than the first.
My gentle lord, bespeak these nobles fair
That wait attendance for a gracious look,
And on their knees salute your majesty.   340

[*The* NOBLES *kneel*]

EDWARD

Courageous Lancaster, embrace thy King,
And as gross vapours perish by the sun,
Even so let hatred with thy sovereign's smile;
Live thou with me as my companion.

LANCASTER

This salutation overjoys my heart.   345

EDWARD

Warwick, shall be my chiefest counsellor:
These silver hairs will more adorn my court
Than gaudy silks or rich embroidery.
Chide me, sweet Warwick, if I go astray.

WARWICK

Slay me, my lord, when I offend your grace.   350

EDWARD

In solemn triumphs and in public shows
Pembroke shall bear the sword before the King.

PEMBROKE

And with this sword Pembroke will fight for you.

EDWARD

But wherefore walks young Mortimer aside?
Be thou commander of our royal fleet,   355
Or if that lofty office like thee not,

338   *bespeak* speak to.
342   *gross vapours* thick mists, fog.
348   *gaudy* ornate.
351   *triumphs . . . public shows* pageants, processions, public entertainments.
352   *bear the sword* The sword of state symbolized justice and was carried at the front of
        processions before the monarch.
354   *aside* (i) to one side (ii) apart, away from a group.
356   *like* please.

I make thee here Lord Marshal of the realm.

MORTIMER JUNIOR

My lord, I'll marshal so your enemies
As England shall be quiet and you safe.

EDWARD

And as for you, Lord Mortimer of Chirke,   360
Whose great achievements in our foreign war
Deserves no common place nor mean reward,
Be you the general of the levied troops
That now are ready to assail the Scots.

MORTIMER SENIOR

In this your grace hath highly honoured me,   365
For with my nature war doth best agree.

ISABELLA

Now is the King of England rich and strong,
Having the love of his renownèd peers.

EDWARD

Ay, Isabel, ne'er was my heart so light.
Clerk of the Crown, direct our warrant forth   370
For Gaveston to Ireland; Beaumont, fly
As fast as Iris or Jove's Mercury.

BEAUMONT

It shall be done, my gracious lord.
                    [*Exit* BEAUMONT, *with the* CLERK OF THE CROWN]

EDWARD

Lord Mortimer, we leave you to your charge.
Now let us in and feast it royally   375
Against our friend the Earl of Cornwall comes.
We'll have a general tilt and tournament,
And then his marriage shall be solemnized;
For wot you not that I have made him sure
Unto our cousin, the Earl of Gloucester's heir?   380

360   *Chirke* i.e. Mortimer Senior, whose estate bordered Shropshire and Wales.
370   *Clerk of the Crown* an officer of Chancery responsible for framing and issuing writs
       of various sorts in both the House of Lords and the House of Commons.
372   *Iris . . . Mercury* In classical mythology, Iris was the rainbow and the messenger of
       the gods; Mercury also served the latter function.
376   *Against* until.
377   *tilt* joust.
379   *sure* betrothed.
380   *Earl of Gloucester's heir* i.e. Lady Margaret de Clare.

LANCASTER

Such news we hear, my lord.

EDWARD

That day, if not for him, yet for my sake,
Who in the triumph will be challenger,
Spare for no cost; we will requite your love.

WARWICK

In this, or aught, your highness shall command us.   385

EDWARD

Thanks, gentle Warwick; come, let's in and revel.
                              Exeunt [all, except the MORTIMERS]

MORTIMER SENIOR

Nephew, I must to Scotland; thou stayest here.
Leave now to oppose thyself against the King;
Thou seest by nature he is mild and calm,
And seeing his mind so dotes on Gaveston,   390
Let him without controlment have his will.
The mightiest kings have had their minions:
Great Alexander loved Hephaestion;
The conquering Hercules for Hylas wept;
And for Patroclus stern Achilles drooped.   395
And not kings only, but the wisest men:
The Roman Tully loved Octavius,
Grave Socrates, wild Alcibiades.
Then let his grace, whose youth is flexible
And promiseth as much as we can wish,   400

386   sd ed. (*Manent* Mortimers. Q).

391   *controlment* restraint.

393   *Great Alexander ... Hephaestion* Alexander III of Macedon (356–323 BC), the celebrated ruler, had an intimate friendship with the military commander Hephaestion (d. 325 BC).

394   *Hercules* ed. (*Hector* Q). See 1.143. It seems unlikely that Marlowe would here bungle a classical reference which he got right in an earlier scene; and the emended line is metrically superior if the word 'conquering' is disyllabic, as it usually is in Marlowe's verse.

395   *Achilles* in classical mythology, the Greek warrior who murdered Hector in the Trojan Wars following the death of Patroclus, his closest companion. This narrative is best known in Homer's *Iliad* and was later dramatized by Shakespeare in *Troilus and Cressida*, which intimates a homosexual relationship between the two warriors.

397   *Tully* Marcus Tullius Cicero (106–43 BC), the Roman statesman. Octavius Caesar (63 BC–AD 14), however, did not have any particular relationship with Cicero.

398   *Socrates* Greek philosopher (469–399 BC).
       Alcibiades Athenian politician (*c.* 450–404 BC) and pupil of Socrates, renowned for his beauty.

Freely enjoy that vain light-headed Earl,
For riper years will wean him from such toys.
MORTIMER JUNIOR
Uncle, his wanton humour grieves not me,
But this I scorn, that one so basely born
Should by his sovereign's favour grow so pert,   405
And riot it with the treasure of the realm
While soldiers mutiny for want of pay.
He wears a lord's revenue on his back,
And Midas-like he jets it in the court
With base outlandish cullions at his heels,   410
Whose proud fantastic liveries make such show
As if that Proteus, god of shapes, appeared.
I have not seen a dapper jack so brisk;
He wears a short Italian hooded cloak,
Larded with pearl; and in his Tuscan cap   415
A jewel of more value than the crown.
Whiles other walk below, the King and he
From out a window laugh at such as we,
And flout our train and jest at our attire.
Uncle, 'tis this that makes me impatient.   420
MORTIMER SENIOR
But nephew, now you see the King is changed.
MORTIMER JUNIOR
Then so am I, and live to do him service;

402   *toys* trifles.
408   *wears . . . back* proverbial (Tilley L 452). Cf. *2 Henry VI,* 'She bears a duke's revenues on her back' (I.iii.83).
409   *Midas* king of Phrygia who was granted the power to turn all that he touched to gold. Cf. Ovid's *Metamorphoses,* XI. 92 ff.
       jets it struts.
410   *outlandish* foreign.
       cullions low fellows.
412   *Proteus* sea god who had the ability to change shape. Cf. Ovid's *Metamorphoses,* VIII. 730–7.
413   *dapper jack* fashionable gentleman.
       brisk smartly dressed.
414–15 Gaveston's taste in clothes serves to emphasize his homosexuality, thought by the Elizabethans to be a particularly Italian vice.
415   *Larded* excessively decorated.
       Tuscan cap a fashionable hat from Tuscany, made from finely woven straw.
417   *other* others.
419   *flout* mock.
       train attendants.

But whiles I have a sword, a hand, a heart,
I will not yield to any such upstart.
You know my mind. Come, uncle, let's away.   425

Exeunt

[SCENE 5]

Enter SPENCER [JUNIOR] *and* BALDOCK

BALDOCK

Spencer,
Seeing that our lord th' Earl of Gloucester's dead,
Which of the nobles dost thou mean to serve?

SPENCER JUNIOR

Not Mortimer, nor any of his side,
Because the King and he are enemies.   5
Baldock, learn this of me: a factious lord
Shall hardly do himself good, much less us;
But he that hath the favour of a king
May with one word advance us while we live.
The liberal Earl of Cornwall is the man   10
On whose good fortune Spencer's hope depends.

BALDOCK

What, mean you then to be his follower?

SPENCER JUNIOR

No, his companion; for he loves me well
And would have once preferred me to the King.

BALDOCK

But he is banished; there's small hope of him.   15

SPENCER JUNIOR

Ay, for a while; but, Baldock, mark the end:
A friend of mine told me in secrecy

1–2   ed. (*Spencer,* seeing . . . Glo- / sters dead, Q).
6   *factious* seditious.
10   *liberal* (i) one who displays the qualities of a gentleman (ii) one who behaves licen-
       tiously.
12   *follower* retainer.
14   *preferred . . . to* (i) recommended to (ii) favoured more than (i.e. sexually).
16   *end* conclusion.

That he's repealed and sent for back again;
And even now, a post came from the court
With letters to our lady from the King,   20
And as she read, she smiled, which makes me think
It is about her lover, Gaveston.

BALDOCK

'Tis like enough, for since he was exiled,
She neither walks abroad nor comes in sight.
But I had thought the match had been broke off   25
And that his banishment had changed her mind.

SPENCER JUNIOR

Our lady's first love is not wavering;
My life for thine, she will have Gaveston.

BALDOCK

Then hope I by her means to be preferred,
Having read unto her since she was a child.   30

SPENCER JUNIOR

Then, Baldock, you must cast the scholar off
And learn to court it like a gentleman.
'Tis not a black coat and a little band,
A velvet-caped cloak, faced before with serge,
And smelling to a nosegay all the day,   35
Or holding of a napkin in your hand,
Or saying a long grace at a table's end,

---

20   *our lady* i.e. Margaret de Clare, daughter of the dead Earl of Gloucester.

28   *My life.. . thine* proverbial (Dent L 260.1).

30   *Having read unto her* Baldock, an Oxford scholar, is portrayed as Margaret de Clare's tutor.

31   *cast the scholar off* i.e. cease to behave like an academic.

32   *court it* behave like a courtier.

33–4   Spencer Junior 'gives a thumbnail sketch of the typical poor scholar who failed to achieve academic preferment and was compelled to take up duties in a nobleman's household, tutoring the children and acting as domestic chaplain' (Gill). Many editors cite John Earle's 'A young raw Preacher' in his *Micro-cosmographie* (1628), 'His fashion and demure habit gets him in with some town-precisian, and makes him a guest on Friday nights. You shall know him by his narrow veluet cape, and serge facing, and his ruffe, next his haire, the shortest thing about him' (Sig. B4[V]).

33   *black coat . . . little band* subfusc or academic dress.

34   *faced* trimmed, patched.
      serge cheap woollen material.

35   *nosegay* posy, bunch of flowers.

37   *table's end* the bottom end of the table (below the salt), which signified the lowest position of social status.

Or making low legs to a nobleman,
Or looking downward, with your eyelids close,
And saying, 'Truly, an't may please your honour',   40
Can get you any favour with great men.
You must be proud, bold, pleasant, resolute,
And now and then, stab, as occasion serves.

BALDOCK

Spencer, thou knowest I hate such formal toys,
And use them but of mere hypocrisy.   45
Mine old lord, whiles he lived, was so precise
That he would take exceptions at my buttons,
And, being like pins' heads, blame me for the bigness,
Which made me curate-like in mine attire,
Though inwardly licentious enough   50
And apt for any kind of villainy.
I am none of these common pedants, I,
That cannot speak without '*propterea quod*'.

SPENCER JUNIOR

But one of those that saith '*quandoquidem*'
And hath a special gift to form a verb.   55

BALDOCK

Leave off this jesting – here my lady comes.

[*They withdraw*]

38   *low legs* deferential, obeisant bowing
40   *an't* if it.
42   *pleasant* jocular.
43   *stab* with pun on sexual thrusting.
44   *formal toys* trivial formalities, conventions.
46   *old* former.
      whiles while.
      precise punctilious, puritanical.
47   *take exceptions at* find fault with.
50   *licentious* (i) unrestrained, indecorous (ii) given to sexual licence.
51   *apt* ready, prepared.
52   *common* ordinary.
      pedants ed. (pendants Q; pedants Q2–4) schoolmasters, tutors
53, 54   *propterea quod, quandoquidem* Even though both expressions mean 'because', the
      former phrase (as suggested by Briggs) is prosaic and less refined than the verse of
      'quandoquidem'; perhaps varsity humour is implied. Arguably, the use of Latin
      ridicules the affected rhetoric of scholarship.
55   *to form* to conjugate.
56   *off* ed. (of Q).
56   sd 1 *They withdraw* They move to the side of the stage, and Lady Margaret is appar-
      ently unaware of their presence, watching and overhearing her.

Enter the LADY [MARGARET DE CLARE, *with letters*]

LADY MARGARET

    The grief for his exile was not so much

    As is the joy of his returning home.

    This letter came from my sweet Gaveston.   [*She reads the letter*]

    What needst thou love, thus to excuse thyself?   60

    I know thou couldst not come and visit me.

    'I will not long be from thee, though I die':

    This argues the entire love of my lord;

    'When I forsake thee, death seize on my heart.'

    But rest thee here where Gaveston shall sleep.   65

                    [*She places the letter in her bosom*]

    Now to the letter of my lord the King.

                        [*She reads another letter*]

    He wills me to repair unto the court

    And meet my Gaveston. Why do I stay,

    Seeing that he talks thus of my marriage-day?

    Who's there? Baldock?   70

    [BALDOCK *and* SPENCER JUNIOR *come forward*]

    See that my coach be ready; I must hence.

BALDOCK

    It shall be done, madam.

LADY MARGARET

    And meet me at the park pale presently.

                            Exit [BALDOCK]

    Spencer, stay you and bear me company,

    For I have joyful news to tell thee of.   75

    My lord of Cornwall is a-coming over

    And will be at the court as soon as we.

SPENCER JUNIOR

    I knew the King would have him home again.

LADY MARGARET

    If all things sort out, as I hope they will,

    Thy service, Spencer, shall be thought upon.   80

67   *repair* come.

71   *coach* In fact, coaches were not ordinarily used in England until after 1564.

73   *park pale* the fencing of an estate or park.
      presently directly.

73   sd ed. (*Exit.* Q after 'madam', line 72).

74   *bear me company* i.e. keep me company.

SPENCER JUNIOR

    I humbly thank your ladyship.

LADY MARGARET

    Come, lead the way; I long till I am there.

                                        [Exeunt]

[SCENE 6]

Enter EDWARD, [ISABELLA] *the Queen,* LANCASTER,
MORTIMER [JUNIOR], WARWICK, PEMBROKE,
KENT, *attendants*

EDWARD

    The wind is good, I wonder why he stays.

    I fear me he is wrecked upon the sea.

ISABELLA

    Look, Lancaster, how passionate he is,

    And still his mind runs on his minion.

LANCASTER

    My lord –   5

EDWARD

    How now, what news? Is Gaveston arrived?

MORTIMER JUNIOR

    Nothing but Gaveston! What means your grace?

    You have matters of more weight to think upon;

    The King of France sets foot in Normandy.

EDWARD

    A trifle! We'll expel him when we please.   10

    But tell me, Mortimer, what's thy device

    Against the stately triumph we decreed?

MORTIMER JUNIOR

    A homely one, my lord, not worth the telling.

  82   *long* am restless.

    3   *passionate* grief-stricken, sorrowful.
    4   *runs on* is preoccupied with.
    9   Normandy was part of English crown territory; cf. 11.64.
  11   *device* an heraldic emblem (painted on a shield).
  12   *Against* prepared for.
        triumph public entertainment, pageant, festival.
  13   *homely* plain, not ostentatious.

EDWARD

    Prithee let me know it.

MORTIMER JUNIOR

    But seeing you are so desirous, thus it is: 15

    A lofty cedar tree fair flourishing,

    On whose top branches kingly eagles perch,

    And by the bark a canker creeps me up

    And gets unto the highest bough of all;

    The motto: *Æque tandem.*   20

EDWARD

    And what is yours, my lord of Lancaster?

LANCASTER

    My lord, mine's more obscure than Mortimer's:

    Pliny reports there is a flying fish

    Which all the other fishes deadly hate,

    And therefore, being pursued, it takes the air;   25

    No sooner is it up, but there's a fowl

    That seizeth it. This fish, my lord, I bear;

    The motto this: *Undique mors est.*

EDWARD

    Proud Mortimer! Ungentle Lancaster!

    Is this the love you bear your sovereign?   30

    Is this the fruit your reconcilement bears?

    Can you in words make show of amity,

    And in your shields display your rancorous minds?

    What call you this but private libelling

    Against the Earl of Cornwall and my brother?   35

16   *lofty* A latent double meaning implies Gaveston's arrogance.
      cedar tree symbol of the structure of society with the king represented by the highest bough.

18   *canker* worm which consumes plants.
      creeps me up creeps up.

20   *Æque tandem* (Latin) Equal in height. Mortimer Junior is suggesting that Gaveston is the canker which is infecting the state, moving from the base (i.e. the commons) to the top (i.e. the nobility).

21   *yours* i.e. the device on Lancaster's shield.

22   *obscure* hard to interpret.

23   *Pliny* Gaius Plinius Secundus or Pliny the Elder (AD 23/4–79), Roman scholar and naturalist best known for his *Naturalis Historia* (AD 77).

28   *Undique mors est* (Latin) Death is on all sides.

31   *reconcilement* reconciliation.

34   *libelling* Rowland points out that this is an anachronism: 'libel in the sense of a defamatory document or statement was a sixteenth-century development'.

35   *my brother* i.e. Gaveston.

ISABELLA

Sweet husband, be content; they all love you.

EDWARD

They love me not that hate my Gaveston.
I am that cedar; shake me not too much.
And you the eagles; soar ye ne'er so high,
I have the jesses that will pull you down,   40
And '*Æque tandem*' shall that canker cry
Unto the proudest peer of Britainy.
Though thou compar'st him to a flying fish,
And threatenest death whether he rise or fall,
'Tis not the hugest monster of the sea   45
Nor foulest harpy that shall swallow him.

MORTIMER JUNIOR [*To the* NOBLES]

If in his absence thus he favours him,
What will he do whenas he shall be present?

Enter GAVESTON

LANCASTER

That shall we see: look where his lordship comes.

EDWARD

My Gaveston!   50
Welcome to Tynemouth, welcome to thy friend.
Thy absence made me droop and pine away;
For as the lovers of fair Danaë,
When she was locked up in a brazen tower,
Desired her more and waxed outrageous,   55
So did it sure with me; and now thy sight

---

40   *jesses* (gresses Q) straps which were fastened to the legs of hawks.

42   *Britainy* Britain (England and Scotland).

43–6 Edward draws upon the images of the flying fish and the fowl (from Lancaster's
      description of his device) and exaggerates them in order to undermine the verbal
      assaults of the two nobles.

46   *harpy* in classical mythology, bird-like creatures with female faces and breasts, which
      stole food and harassed Phineus, the blind King of Thrace, when he entertained the
      Argonauts.

48   *whenas* when.

48   sd ed.; after line 49 in Q.

53   *Danaë* In classical mythology, she was incarcerated by her father in a bronze tower
      after an oracle prophesied that her son would murder him; Jupiter then visited her
      in a shower of gold and she conceived the hero Perseus.

55   *waxed* grew.
      outrageous unrestrained (four syllables).

Is sweeter far than was thy parting hence
Bitter and irksome to my sobbing heart.

GAVESTON

Sweet lord and King, your speech preventeth mine.
Yet have I words left to express my joy: 60
The shepherd nipped with biting winter's rage
Frolics not more to see the painted spring
Than I do to behold your majesty.

EDWARD

Will none of you salute my Gaveston?

LANCASTER

Salute him? Yes! Welcome, Lord Chamberlain.   65

MORTIMER JUNIOR

Welcome is the good Earl of Cornwall.

WARWICK

Welcome, Lord Governor of the Isle of Man.

PEMBROKE

Welcome, Master Secretary.

KENT

Brother, do you hear them?

EDWARD

Still will these earls and barons use me thus!   70

GAVESTON

My lord, I cannot brook these injuries.

ISABELLA [*Aside*]

Ay me, poor soul, when these begin to jar.

EDWARD

Return it to their throats; I'll be thy warrant.

GAVESTON

Base leaden earls that glory in your birth,
Go sit at home and eat your tenants' beef,   75

59   *preventeth* anticipates.
62   *painted* colourful, decorated with flowers.
70   *use* behave towards, treat.
72   *jar* quarrel, wrangle.
73   *Return . . . throats* i.e. reject their abuse, 'give them the lie' (a provocative act,
      normally a formal challenge to a duel); cf. Shakespeare, *Titus Andronicus*, II.i.53–6.
      warrant document of authorization.
74   *Base leaden* Gaveston likens the nobles to the dullness of cheap alloy coins, with a
      latent pun on the name of a gold coin, a 'noble'.
75   *eat . . . beef* an insult, implying that the nobles are 'beef-witted' (stupid, brainless).
      Forker suggests that Frenchmen such as Gaveston regarded the English as great
      eaters of beef.

And come not here to scoff at Gaveston,
Whose mounting thoughts did never creep so low
As to bestow a look on such as you.

LANCASTER

Yet I disdain not to do this for you.   *[Draws his sword]*

EDWARD

Treason, treason! Where's the traitor?

PEMBROKE *[indicating GAVESTON]*

                    Here, here!   80

EDWARD

Convey hence Gaveston; they'll murder him.

GAVESTON

The life of thee shall salve this foul disgrace.

MORTIMER JUNIOR

Villain, thy life, unless I miss mine aim.

                      [He wounds GAVESTON]

ISABELLA

Ah, furious Mortimer, what hast thou done?

MORTIMER JUNIOR

No more than I would answer were he slain.   85

                   [Exit GAVESTON, attended]

EDWARD

Yes, more than thou canst answer, though he live;
Dear shall you both aby this riotous deed.
Out of my presence! Come not near the court.

MORTIMER JUNIOR

I'll not be barred the court for Gaveston.

LANCASTER

We'll hale him by the ears unto the block.   90

EDWARD

Look to your own heads; his is sure enough.

---

79   sd: It was an offence to brandish weapons in the King's presence.
80–1   ed. Q erroneously prints Edward's line and speech prefix as part of Pembroke's dialogue. (Heere here King: conuey . . . thaile / murder him.).
82   *salve* atone, remedy (vindication is implied).
85   *answer* answer for.
87   *both* i.e. Mortimer Junior and Lancaster.
       aby pay for, atone.
       riotous wanton, amoral.
90   *hale* drag, pull (forcibly).
91   *sure* safe.

WARWICK

Look to your own crown, if you back him thus.

KENT

Warwick, these words do ill beseem thy years.

EDWARD

Nay, all of them conspire to cross me thus;
But if I live, I'll tread upon their heads   95
That think with high looks thus to tread me down.
Come, Edmund, let's away and levy men;
'Tis war that must abate these barons' pride.

Exit [EDWARD] *the King*[, *with* ISABELLA *and* KENT]

WARWICK

Let's to our castles, for the King is moved.

MORTIMER JUNIOR

Moved may he be and perish in his wrath.   100

LANCASTER

Cousin, it is no dealing with him now.
He means to make us stoop by force of arms,
And therefore let us jointly here protest
To prosecute that Gaveston to the death.

MORTIMER JUNIOR

By heaven, the abject villain shall not live.   105

WARWICK

I'll have his blood or die in seeking it.

PEMBROKE

The like oath Pembroke takes.

LANCASTER   And so doth Lancaster.
Now send our heralds to defy the King
And make the people swear to put him down.

Enter a POST

93   *ill beseem . . . years* i.e. you should display greater wisdom and prudence, considering
      your age.
94   *cross* obstruct, thwart.
101   *Cousin* used more broadly than in modern English, to denote a variety of kin-
      ship and other associations.
      it is there is.
102   *stoop* submit.
103   *protest* vow.
104   *prosecute* pursue.
105   *abject* most contemptible, servile.
108   *heralds* messengers or officials used in time of war to carry messages to the enemy.
109   sd POST messenger.

MORTIMER JUNIOR

Letters? From whence? 110

POST

From Scotland, my lord.

LANCASTER

Why how now, cousin, how fares all our friends?

MORTIMER JUNIOR [*Reading a letter*]

My uncle's taken prisoner by the Scots.

LANCASTER

We'll have him ransomed, man; be of good cheer.

MORTIMER JUNIOR

They rate his ransom at five thousand pound. 115
Who should defray the money but the King,
Seeing he is taken prisoner in his wars?
I'll to the King.

LANCASTER

Do cousin, and I'll bear thee company.

WARWICK

Meantime, my lord of Pembroke and myself 120
Will to Newcastle here and gather head.

MORTIMER JUNIOR

About it then, and we will follow you.

LANCASTER

Be resolute and full of secrecy.

WARWICK

I warrant you.

[*Exeunt all but* MORTIMER JUNIOR *and* LANCASTER]

MORTIMER JUNIOR

Cousin, an if he will not ransom him, 125
I'll thunder such a peal into his ears
As never subject did unto his king.

LANCASTER

Content; I'll bear my part. Holla! Who's there?

[*Enter a* GUARD]

---

111   sp POST ed. (*Messen.* Q).
116   *defray* pay for, settle the payment.
121   *gather head* raise forces.
123   *resolute* determined.
124   *warrant* give assurance.
128   *Content* agreed.

MORTIMER JUNIOR

    Ay, marry, such a guard as this doth well.

LANCASTER

    Lead on the way.

GUARD   Whither will your lordships?   130

MORTIMER JUNIOR

    Whither else but to the King?

GUARD

    His highness is disposed to be alone.

LANCASTER

    Why, so he may, but we will speak to him.

GUARD

    You may not in, my lord.

MORTIMER JUNIOR

    May we not?   135

            [Enter EDWARD *and* KENT]

EDWARD

    How now, what noise is this?

    Who have we there? Is't you?

                     [He makes to exit, ignoring MORTIMER JUNIOR

                                     and LANCASTER]

MORTIMER JUNIOR

    Nay, stay, my lord; I come to bring you news:

    Mine uncle's taken prisoner by the Scots.

EDWARD

    Then ransom him.   140

LANCASTER

    'Twas in your wars: you should ransom him.

MORTIMER JUNIOR

    And you shall ransom him, or else –

KENT

    What, Mortimer, you will not threaten him?

EDWARD

    Quiet yourself; you shall have the broad seal

---

129   *marry* to be sure (contracted form of the affirmation 'By Mary').

134   *in* i.e. enter the king's chamber.

144   *broad seal* letters patent giving the bearer the right to raise money for a specific purpose without being prosecuted for begging. Edward's offer insultingly implies that Mortimer Junior is impoverished.

To gather for him thoroughout the realm.   145
LANCASTER
Your minion Gaveston hath taught you this.
MORTIMER JUNIOR
My lord, the family of the Mortimers
Are not so poor but, would they sell their land,
Would levy men enough to anger you.
We never beg, but use such prayers as these.   150
                    [*He puts his hand on the hilt of his sword*]
EDWARD
Shall I still be haunted thus?
MORTIMER JUNIOR
Nay, now you are here alone, I'll speak my mind.
LANCASTER
And so will I; and then, my lord, farewell.
MORTIMER JUNIOR
The idle triumphs, masques, lascivious shows,
And prodigal gifts bestowed on Gaveston   155
Have drawn thy treasure dry and made thee weak;
The murmuring commons overstretched hath.
LANCASTER
Look for rebellion, look to be deposed:
Thy garrisons are beaten out of France,
And, lame and poor, lie groaning at the gates;   160
The wild O'Neill, with swarms of Irish kerns,
Lives uncontrolled within the English pale;
Unto the walls of York the Scots made road

145   *gather* collect money.
        thoroughout throughout.
151   *haunted* persistently molested.
154   *idle* vain, worthless.
155   *prodigal* lavish, extravagant.
156   *drawn* emptied, drained.
        treasure treasury.
157   *murmuring* discontented, disgruntled.
        commons the common people.
        overstretched i.e. created an intolerable strain.
161   *The . . . O'Neill* prominent Ulster clan chieftain, not mentioned in the sources. In
        1592, the title was contested; it was conferred on Hugh O'Neill, 2nd Earl of Tyrone,
        in May 1593.
        Irish kerns footsoldiers, commonly recruited from the poorer class of the 'wild Irish'.
162   *English pale* an area of land around Dublin established for the protection of English
        settlers.
163   *made road* raided.

And, unresisted, drave away rich spoils.

MORTIMER JUNIOR

    The haughty Dane commands the narrow seas,   165

    While in the harbour ride thy ships unrigged.

LANCASTER

    What foreign prince sends thee ambassadors?

MORTIMER JUNIOR

    Who loves thee but a sort of flatterers?

LANCASTER

    Thy gentle Queen, sole sister to Valois,

    Complains that thou hast left her all forlorn.   170

MORTIMER JUNIOR

    Thy court is naked, being bereft of those

    That makes a king seem glorious to the world –

    I mean the peers whom thou shouldst dearly love.

    Libels are cast again thee in the street,

    Ballads and rhymes made of thy overthrow.   175

LANCASTER

    The northern borderers, seeing their houses burnt,

    Their wives and children slain, run up and down

    Cursing the name of thee and Gaveston.

MORTIMER JUNIOR

    When wert thou in the field with banner spread?

    But once! And then thy soldiers marched like players,   180

    With garish robes, not armour; and thyself,

    Bedaubed with gold, rode laughing at the rest,

164   *drave* drove.

        spoils plunder, booty.

165   *the narrow seas* the English Channel.

166   *ride* lie at anchor.

        unrigged without their rigging.

168   *sort* group.

169   *Valois* i.e. Philip, King of France (family name).

170   *forlorn* desolate, abandoned.

171   *naked* destitute.

172   *seem* appear.

174   *Libels* subversive pamphlets.

        again against.

175   *Ballads and rhymes* In Elizabethan England these were the cheapest and most demotic form of literature, costing one penny.

176   *their* ed. (the Q).

180   *players* actors.

Nodding and shaking of thy spangled crest
Where women's favours hung like labels down.

LANCASTER

And thereof came it that the fleering Scots,   185
To England's high disgrace, have made this jig:
   'Maids of England, sore may you mourn,
For your lemans you have lost at Bannockburn.
   With a heave and a ho.
What weeneth the King of England,   190
   So soon to have won Scotland?
   With a rumbelow.'

MORTIMER JUNIOR

Wigmore shall fly, to set my uncle free.

LANCASTER

And when 'tis gone, our swords shall purchase more.
If ye be moved, revenge it as you can;   195
Look next to see us with our ensigns spread.
     Exeunt NOBLES [LANCASTER *and* MORTIMER JUNIOR]

EDWARD

My swelling heart for very anger breaks!
How oft have I been baited by these peers
And dare not be revenged, for their power is great?
Yet, shall the crowing of these cockerels   200
Affright a lion? Edward, unfold thy paws
And let their lives' blood slake thy fury's hunger.
If I be cruel and grow tyrannous,

---

183   *crest* the plume or decoration on the top of a helmet.
184   *favours* tokens of affection or keepsakes (gloves, scarves) given by ladies to knights
and worn either in battle or in a tournament.
     labels slips of paper or parchment for attaching seals to documents.
185   *fleering* sneering, jeering.
186   *jig* insulting song or ballad.
188   *lemans* sweethearts.
     Bannockburn The battle of Bannockburn (24 June 1314) ended in the defeat of
Edward's forces following an attempt to secure Stirling Castle from the Scots. The
Q spelling, 'Bannocksborne', emphasizes the rhyme.
190   *weeneth* hopes, expects.
192   *rumbelow* meaningless refrain which maintains the rhyme of the song.
193   *Wigmore* Wigmore Castle (Mortimer Junior's Herefordshire estate).
     shall fly i.e. shall be sold.
194   *purchase* earn, acquire.
196   *ensigns* banners (displayed by each side in battle).
200–1 *cockerels . . . lion* The lion was, in fact, proverbially afraid of the cock's crowing; see
MLN 50 (1935), 352–4.

Now let them thank themselves and rue too late.

KENT

My lord, I see your love to Gaveston   205
Will be the ruin of the realm and you,
For now the wrathful nobles threaten wars;
And therefore, brother, banish him forever.

EDWARD

Art thou an enemy to my Gaveston?

KENT

Ay, and it grieves me that I favoured him.   210

EDWARD

Traitor, be gone; whine thou with Mortimer.

KENT

So will I, rather than with Gaveston.

EDWARD

Out of my sight, and trouble me no more.

KENT

No marvel though thou scorn thy noble peers,
When I thy brother am rejected thus.   215

EDWARD

Away!

Exit [KENT]

Poor Gaveston, that hast no friend but me.
Do what they can, we'll live in Tynemouth here,
And, so I walk with him about the walls,
What care I though the earls begirt us round?   220

Enter [ISABELLA] *the Queen, three ladies*
[MARGARET DE CLARE *with two ladies in waiting,*
GAVESTON], BALDOCK, *and* SPENCER [JUNIOR]

Here comes she that's cause of all these jars.

ISABELLA

My lord, 'tis thought the earls are up in arms.

EDWARD

Ay, and 'tis likewise thought you favour him.

ISABELLA

Thus do you still suspect me without cause.

216–17   ed. (*one line in* Q).
   220   *begirt* surround, enclose.
   220   sd ed. (after 221 in Q: *Enter the Queens, Ladies 3, Baldock, / and Spencer.*)
   223   *him* Mortimer Junior; Edward is more preoccupied with personal than political
         betrayal.

55

LADY MARGARET

   Sweet uncle, speak more kindly to the Queen. 225

GAVESTON [*Aside to* EDWARD]

   My lord, dissemble with her, speak her fair.

EDWARD

   Pardon me, sweet, I forgot myself.

ISABELLA

   Your pardon is quickly got of Isabel.

EDWARD

   The younger Mortimer is grown so brave

   That to my face he threatens civil wars. 230

GAVESTON

   Why do you not commit him to the Tower?

EDWARD

   I dare not, for the people love him well.

GAVESTON

   Why then, we'll have him privily made away.

EDWARD

   Would Lancaster and he had both caroused

   A bowl of poison to each other's health. 235

   But let them go, and tell me what are these?

LADY MARGARET

   Two of my father's servants whilst he lived;

   May't please your grace to entertain them now.

EDWARD

   Tell me, where wast thou born? What is thine arms?

BALDOCK

   My name is Baldock, and my gentry 240

   I fetched from Oxford, not from heraldry.

---

226   *fair* courteously.
229   *brave* defiant, impertinent.
233   *privily made away* secretly murdered.
234   *caroused* quaffed.
235   *health* well-being, prosperity (with ironic pun on physical health).
236   *let them go* i.e. enough talk of them (Forker).
238   *entertain* take into service, employ.
239   ed. (Tell . . . borne? / What . . . armes? Q).
     arms coat of arms.
240   *gentry* rank (of a gentleman).
241   *fetched . . . Oxford* The status of a gentleman could be acquired through having been educated at Oxford.
     heraldry heraldic title, rank.

EDWARD

    The fitter art thou, Baldock, for my turn;

    Wait on me, and I'll see thou shalt not want.

BALDOCK

    I humbly thank your majesty.

EDWARD

    Knowest thou him, Gaveston?

GAVESTON   Ay, my lord.   245

    His name is Spencer; he is well allied.

    For my sake let him wait upon your grace;

    Scarce shall you find a man of more desert.

EDWARD

    Then, Spencer, wait upon me; for his sake

    I'll grace thee with a higher style ere long.   250

SPENCER JUNIOR

    No greater titles happen unto me

    Than to be favoured of your majesty.

EDWARD [*To* LADY MARGARET]

    Cousin, this day shall be your marriage feast.

    And, Gaveston, think that I love thee well

    To wed thee to our niece, the only heir   255

    Unto the Earl of Gloucester late deceased.

GAVESTON

    I know, my lord, many will stomach me,

    But I respect neither their love nor hate.

EDWARD

    The headstrong barons shall not limit me;

    He that I list to favour shall be great.   260

    Come, let's away; and when the marriage ends,

    Have at the rebels and their complices.

                                   Exeunt

245–6   ed. (*Edw.* Knowest . . . *Gaueston? I Gau.* I . . . alied, Q).

246   *well allied* well connected, of good birth.

250   *style* title, status.

251   *happen unto me* i.e. could befall me.

252   *of* by.

253   *Cousin* Cf. 101 n. above.

257   *stomach* resent.

260   *list* choose.

262   *Have at* attack.

       complices confederates.

[SCENE 7]

Enter LANCASTER, MORTIMER [JUNIOR],
WARWICK, PEMBROKE, KENT

KENT

My lords, of love to this our native land
I come to join with you and leave the King;
And in your quarrel and the realm's behoof
Will be the first that shall adventure life.

LANCASTER

I fear me you are sent of policy   5
To undermine us with a show of love.

WARWICK

He is your brother; therefore have we cause
To cast the worst and doubt of your revolt.

KENT

Mine honour shall be hostage of my truth;
If that will not suffice, farewell, my lords.   10

MORTIMER JUNIOR

Stay, Edmund; never was Plantagenet
False of his word, and therefore trust we thee.

PEMBROKE

But what's the reason you should leave him now?

KENT

I have informed the Earl of Lancaster.

LANCASTER

And it sufficeth. Now, my lords, know this,   15
That Gaveston is secretly arrived,
And here in Tynemouth frolics with the King.
Let us with these our followers scale the walls,
And suddenly surprise them unawares.

---

3   *behoof* benefit.
4   *adventure* risk.
5   *of policy* i.e. out of deceit, under false pretences.
8   *cast* reckon, fear.
     doubt of suspect.
17   *frolics* makes merry (the verb also has sexual connotations).

MORTIMER JUNIOR
    I'll give the onset.
WARWICK   And I'll follow thee.   20
MORTIMER JUNIOR
    This tattered ensign of my ancestors,
    Which swept the desert shore of that dead sea
    Whereof we got the name of Mortimer,
    Will I advance upon these castle walls.
    Drums strike alarum! Raise them from their sport,   25
    And ring aloud the knell of Gaveston.

                                     [Alarums]

LANCASTER
    None be so hardy as to touch the King;
    But neither spare you Gaveston nor his friends.

                                       Exeunt

[SCENE 8]

Enter [EDWARD] *the King and* SPENCER [JUNIOR;*
from another door enter] to them* GAVESTON[, *unseen by*
EDWARD *and* SPENCER JUNIOR; *with* ISABELLA,
LADY MARGARET DE CLARE, *and attendants*]

EDWARD
    O tell me, Spencer, where is Gaveston?
SPENCER JUNIOR
    I fear me he is slain, my gracious lord.
EDWARD
    No, here he comes! Now let them spoil and kill.

22–3   The Mortimers came from Mortemer in Normandy, and were not, as Marlowe sug-
        gests, connected with the Crusades and the Dead Sea (*Mortuum Mare* in Latin).
24   *these* ed. (this Q). The Q reading could make sense if 'castle' is taken to be a genitive
        with silent final -*s*.
25   *alarum* call to arms, battle-cry.
        sport idle pastimes, amusements.
27   *hardy* bold, reckless.

0   sd ed. (*Enter the king and Spencer, to them / Gaueston, &tc.* Q).
3   *spoil* plunder, destroy.

Fly, fly, my lords; the earls have got the hold.
Take shipping and away to Scarborough;   5
Spencer and I will post away by land.

GAVESTON

Stay, my lord; they will not injure you.

EDWARD

I will not trust them, Gaveston. Away!

GAVESTON

Farewell, my lord.

EDWARD

Lady, farewell.   10

LADY MARGARET

Farewell, sweet uncle, till we meet again.

EDWARD

Farewell, sweet Gaveston, and farewell, niece.

ISABELLA

No farewell to poor Isabel, thy Queen?

EDWARD

Yes, yes – for Mortimer, your lover's sake.

Exeunt [all, except] ISABELLA

ISABELLA

Heavens can witness, I love none but you.   15
From my embracements thus he breaks away;
O that mine arms could close this isle about,
That I might pull him to me where I would,
Or that these tears that drizzle from mine eyes
Had power to mollify his stony heart   20
That when I had him we might never part.

Enter the Barons [LANCASTER, WARWICK,
MORTIMER JUNIOR]

Alarums

LANCASTER

I wonder how he 'scaped?

MORTIMER JUNIOR

Who's this, the Queen?

ISABELLA

Ay, Mortimer, the miserable Queen,

   4   *hold* fortress.
   6   *post* go with speed (by horse).
  14   sd ed. (*Exeunt omnes, manet Isabella.* Q).
  21   sd ed. (*Enter the Barons alarums.* Q).

Whose pining heart, her inward sighs have blasted,   25
And body with continual mourning wasted.
These hands are tired with haling of my lord
From Gaveston, from wicked Gaveston,
And all in vain; for when I speak him fair,
He turns away and smiles upon his minion.   30

MORTIMER JUNIOR
Cease to lament, and tell us where's the King?

ISABELLA
What would you with the King? Is't him you seek?

LANCASTER
No, madam, but that cursed Gaveston.
Far be it from the thought of Lancaster
To offer violence to his sovereign.   35
We would but rid the realm of Gaveston;
Tell us where he remains, and he shall die.

ISABELLA
He's gone by water unto Scarborough.
Pursue him quickly and he cannot 'scape;
The King hath left him, and his train is small.   40

WARWICK
Forslow no time, sweet Lancaster; let's march.

MORTIMER JUNIOR
How comes it that the King and he is parted?

ISABELLA
That this your army, going several ways,
Might be of lesser force, and with the power
That he intendeth presently to raise   45
Be easily suppressed; and therefore be gone.

MORTIMER JUNIOR
Here in the river rides a Flemish hoy;
Let's all aboard and follow him amain.

LANCASTER
The wind that bears him hence will fill our sails.
Come, come aboard – 'tis but an hour's sailing.   50

27   *haling* dragging (forcibly).
40   *train* retinue.
41   *Forslow* waste.
47   *Flemish hoy* small fishing ship used by the Flemings in the North Sea.
48   *amain* with all speed.

MORTIMER JUNIOR

Madam, stay you within this castle here.

ISABELLA

No, Mortimer, I'll to my lord the King.

MORTIMER JUNIOR

Nay, rather sail with us to Scarborough.

ISABELLA

You know the King is so suspicious,
As if he hear I have but talked with you,   55
Mine honour will be called in question;
And therefore, gentle Mortimer, be gone.

MORTIMER JUNIOR

Madam, I cannot stay to answer you;
But think of Mortimer as he deserves.

     [*Exeunt* LANCASTER, WARWICK, *and* MORTIMER JUNIOR]

ISABELLA

So well hast thou deserved, sweet Mortimer,   60
As Isabel could live with thee forever.
In vain I look for love at Edward's hand,
Whose eyes are fixed on none but Gaveston.
Yet once more I'll importune him with prayers;
If he be strange and not regard my words,   65
My son and I will over into France,
And to the King, my brother, there complain
How Gaveston hath robbed me of his love.
But yet I hope my sorrows will have end
And Gaveston this blessed day be slain.   [*Exit*]   70

---

65   *strange* estranged, unresponsive.
70   sd (*Exeunt* Q).

[SCENE 9]

Enter GAVESTON *pursued*

GAVESTON
    Yet, lusty lords, I have escaped your hands,
    Your threats, your 'larums, and your hot pursuits;
    And though divorcèd from King Edward's eyes,
    Yet liveth Piers of Gaveston unsurprised,
    Breathing, in hope (*malgrado* all your beards   5
    That muster rebels thus against your King)
    To see his royal sovereign once again.

Enter the nobles [LANCASTER, WARWICK,
PEMBROKE, MORTIMER JUNIOR, *with soldiers,*
JAMES, HORSE-BOY, *and* PEMBROKE'S MEN]

WARWICK
    Upon him, soldiers! Take away his weapons.

MORTIMER JUNIOR
    Thou proud disturber of thy country's peace,
    Corrupter of thy King, cause of these broils,   10
    Base flatterer, yield! And were it not for shame –
    Shame and dishonour to a soldier's name –
    Upon my weapon's point here shouldst thou fall,
    And welter in thy gore.

LANCASTER   Monster of men,
    That, like the Greekish strumpet, trained to arms   15
    And bloody wars so many valiant knights,

---

    1   *lusty* arrogant, insolent.
    2   *'larums* battle-cries.
    4   *unsurprised* unambushed (and therefore uncaptured).
    5   *malgrado . . . beards* in defiance or direct opposition to your purposes; proverbial
         (Tilley S 764).
  10   *broils* battles.
14–16   ed. (Monster . . . strumpet / Traind . . . warres, / So . . . knights, Q).
  15   *Greekish strumpet* Helen of Troy in Homer's *Iliad,* the great beauty, wife of Menelaus,
         King of Sparta, who fell in love with Paris, son of Priam, King of Troy; she ran away
         with Paris to Troy, and this was the pretext for the Trojan War. Though scornfully
         alluded to here, Helen is elsewhere celebrated in some of Marlowe's most famous
         lines (*Dr Faustus,* A-Text, v.i.90–1).
         trained lured, baited.

Look for no other fortune, wretch, than death;
King Edward is not here to buckler thee.

WARWICK

Lancaster, why talk'st thou to the slave?
Go, soldiers, take him hence; for by my sword,   20
His head shall off. Gaveston, short warning
Shall serve thy turn; it is our country's cause
That here severely we will execute
Upon thy person: hang him at a bough!

GAVESTON

My lord –   25

WARWICK

Soldiers, have him away.
But for thou wert the favourite of a king,
Thou shalt have so much honour at our hands.

                    [*He gestures to indicate beheading*]

GAVESTON

I thank you all, my lords; then I perceive
That heading is one, and hanging is the other,   30
And death is all.

            Enter [LORD MALTRAVERS,] EARL OF ARUNDEL

LANCASTER

How now, my lord of Arundel?

MALTRAVERS

My lords, King Edward greets you all by me.

WARWICK

Arundel, say your message.

MALTRAVERS   His majesty,
Hearing that you had taken Gaveston,   35

---

18   *buckler* shield, protect.
20–2   ed. (Go . . . hence, / For . . . off: / *Gaueston* . . . turne: / It . . . cause, Q).
21   *warning* notice – in this case, of execution, giving the condemned man time to
        prepare himself spiritually. The insinuation that Gaveston needs little time suggests
        the irredeemable state of his soul.
28   *so much honour* Members of the nobility were, by privilege, exempt from hanging.
30   *heading* beheading.
31   *death is all* i.e. death is still the same whether one is beheaded or hanged.
31   sd On the identification of Arundel with Maltravers, see the Note on the Text.
33   sp MALTRAVERS ed. (*Arun.* Q); also at ll. 34 (*Aru.*), 57, 65, 89.
34–5   ed. (*one line in* Q).

Entreateth you by me, that but he may
See him before he dies; for why, he says,
And sends you word, he knows that die he shall;
And if you gratify his grace so far,
He will be mindful of the courtesy.   40

WARWICK
How now?

GAVESTON   Renownèd Edward, how thy name
Revives poor Gaveston.

WARWICK   No, it needeth not.
Arundel, we will gratify the King
In other matters; he must pardon us in this.
Soldiers, away with him.   45

GAVESTON
Why, my lord of Warwick,
Will not these delays beget my hopes?
I know it, lords, it is this life you aim at;
Yet grant King Edward this.

MORTIMER JUNIOR   Shalt thou appoint
What we shall grant? Soldiers, away with him!   50
[*To* MALTRAVERS] Thus we'll gratify the King:
We'll send his head by thee; let him bestow
His tears on that, for that is all he gets
Of Gaveston, or else his senseless trunk.

LANCASTER
Not so, my lord, lest he bestow more cost   55
In burying him than he hath ever earned.

MALTRAVERS
My lords, it is his majesty's request,
And in the honour of a king he swears
He will but talk with him and send him back.

36   *that* ed. (yet Q): the awkward Q reading probably arose from a composito-
      rial misreading of copy 'y^t' (= that).
      but only. Edward is keeping his demands modest.
37   *for why* because.
40   *be mindful* call to mind, take into consideration.
47   *Will . . . hopes?* Gaveston is perturbed that the delay in his execution will not, after
      all, lead to a final meeting with Edward.
48   *aim at* intend (to take).
49–50 ed. (*Mm. iu.* Shalt . . . graunt? / Souldiers . . . him: Q).

WARWICK

When, can you tell? Arundel, no; we wot   60
He that the care of realm remits,
And drives his nobles to these exigents
For Gaveston, will, if he seize him once,
Violate any promise to possess him.

MALTRAVERS

Then if you will not trust his grace in keep,   65
My lords, I will be pledge for his return.

MORTIMER JUNIOR

It is honourable in thee to offer this,
But for we know thou art a noble gentleman,
We will not wrong thee so,
To make away a true man for a thief.   70

GAVESTON

How meanst thou, Mortimer? That is over-base.

MORTIMER JUNIOR

Away, base groom, robber of kings' renown;
Question with thy companions and thy mates.

PEMBROKE

My lord Mortimer, and you my lords each one,
To gratify the King's request therein,   75
Touching the sending of this Gaveston,
Because his majesty so earnestly
Desires to see the man before his death,
I will upon mine honour undertake
To carry him and bring him back again,   80
Provided this, that you, my lord of Arundel
Will join with me.

WARWICK   Pembroke, what wilt thou do?
Cause yet more bloodshed? Is it not enough
That we have taken him, but must we now

60   *wot* know.
61   *remits* surrenders, resigns.
62   *exigents* exigencies, extreme measures.
63   *seize* (zease Q; seaze Q3–4) take possession of.
65   *in keep* i.e. with the loan (i.e. of Gaveston).
66   *pledge* security.
70   *make away* murder (If Gaveston is not returned, Maltravers will be executed in his place.)
73   *Question* argue.
      companions often used as a term of contempt.

Leave him on 'had I wist' and let him go? 85
PEMBROKE
My lords, I will not over-woo your honours,
But if you dare trust Pembroke with the prisoner,
Upon mine oath I will return him back.
MALTRAVERS
My lord of Lancaster, what say you in this?
LANCASTER
Why, I say, let him go on Pembroke's word. 90
PEMBROKE
And you, lord Mortimer?
MORTIMER JUNIOR
How say you, my lord of Warwick?
WARWICK
Nay, do your pleasures; I know how 'twill prove.
PEMBROKE
Then give him me.
GAVESTON   Sweet sovereign, yet I come
To see thee ere I die.
WARWICK [*Aside*]   Yet not perhaps, 95
If Warwick's wit and policy prevail.
MORTIMER JUNIOR
My lord of Pembroke, we deliver him you;
Return him on your honour. Sound away!
            [*Trumpets sound.*] *Exeunt* [*all but*] PEMBROKE,
            MALTRAVERS, GAVESTON *and* PEMBROKE'S MEN,
            four soldiers[*, with* JAMES, *and* HORSE-BOY]
PEMBROKE [*To* MALTRAVERS]
My lord, you shall go with me;
My house is not far hence – out of the way 100
A little – but our men shall go along.
We that have pretty wenches to our wives,
Sir, must not come so near and balk their lips.

85   *'had I wist'* had I known. Proverbial (Tilley H 8).
93   ed. (Nay ... pleasures, / I ... prooue. Q).
      do your pleasures i.e. do as you will.
96   *wit* cunning.
      policy contrivance, stratagem.
98   *Sound away!* He orders a trumpet call signalling a departure.
98   sd ed. (*Exeunt. / Manent Penbrooke, Mat. Gauest & Pen- / brookes men, foure souldiers.* Q).
103   *balk* neglect.

MALTRAVERS

    'Tis very kindly spoke, my lord of Pembroke;

    Your honour hath an adamant of power   105

    To draw a prince.

PEMBROKE   So, my lord. Come hither, James.

    I do commit this Gaveston to thee;

    Be thou this night his keeper. In the morning

    We will discharge thee of thy charge; be gone.

GAVESTON

    Unhappy Gaveston, whither goest thou now?   110

           Exit [GAVESTON, *with* PEMBROKE'S MEN *and* JAMES]

HORSE-BOY

    My lord, we'll quickly be at Cobham.

                      Exeunt [PEMBROKE *and* MALTRAVERS,

                           with the HORSE-BOY *and soldiers*]

[SCENE 10]

Enter GAVESTON *mourning*, [*with* JAMES]
and the EARL OF PEMBROKE'S MEN

GAVESTON

    O treacherous Warwick, thus to wrong thy friend!

JAMES

    I see it is your life these arms pursue.

GAVESTON

    Weaponless must I fall and die in bands.

---

104   *kindly* as befits *either* a nobleman *or* a husband.
105   *adamant* magnet, lodestone.
109   *discharge* relieve.
        charge responsibility.
110   *Unhappy* unfortunate, unlucky.
110   sd ed. (*Exit cum seruis Pen.* Q).
111   *Cobham* small town in Kent, near Gravesend.
111   sd ed. (*Exeunt ambo.* Q).

    1   *wrong thy friend* i.e. betray Pembroke.
    2   *arms* i.e. soldiers.
    3   *bands* bonds, fetters.

O, must this day be period of my life,
Centre of all my bliss? An ye be men,   5
Speed to the King.

Enter WARWICK *and his company*

WARWICK   My lord of Pembroke's men.
Strive you no longer; I will have that Gaveston.

JAMES
Your lordship doth dishonour to yourself
And wrong our lord, your honourable friend.

WARWICK
No, James, it is my country's cause I follow.   10
Go, take the villain; soldiers, come away,
We'll make quick work. Commend me to your master,
My friend, and tell him that I watched it well.
[*To* GAVESTON] Come, let thy shadow parley with King Edward.

GAVESTON
Treacherous Earl, shall I not see the King?   15

WARWICK
The king of heaven perhaps, no other king.
Away!

Exeunt WARWICK *and his men, with* GAVESTON.
JAMES *remains with the others*

JAMES
Come fellows, it booted not for us to strive.
We will in haste go certify our lord.

Exeunt

---

4   *period* the end.
      Centre nadir, the greatest depth (possibly implying the centre of the earth).
6   *Speed* hasten, hurry.
7   *Strive* struggle.
13   *watched it well* i.e. guarded Gaveston efficiently.
14   *shadow* ghost.
17   sd ed. (*Exeunt Warwike and his men, with Gauest. / Manet Iames cum cæteris.* Q).
18   *booted not* was useless.

[SCENE 11]

Enter King EDWARD *and* SPENCER [JUNIOR,
and BALDOCK], *with drums and fifes*

EDWARD

I long to hear an answer from the barons
Touching my friend, my dearest Gaveston.
Ah, Spencer, not the riches of my realm
Can ransom him; ah, he is marked to die.
I know the malice of the younger Mortimer;   5
Warwick, I know, is rough, and Lancaster
Inexorable; and I shall never see
My lovely Piers, my Gaveston, again.
The barons overbear me with their pride.

SPENCER JUNIOR

Were I King Edward, England's sovereign,   10
Son to the lovely Eleanor of Spain,
Great Edward Longshanks' issue, would I bear
These braves, this rage, and suffer uncontrolled
These barons thus to beard me in my land,
In mine own realm? My lord, pardon my speech.   15
Did you retain your father's magnanimity,
Did you regard the honour of your name,
You would not suffer thus your majesty
Be counterbuffed of your nobility.
Strike off their heads, and let them preach on poles;   20
No doubt such lessons they will teach the rest,
As by their preachments they will profit much
And learn obedience to their lawful King.

---

11 *Eleanor of Spain* Eleanor of Castile, first wife of Edward I.
12 *Longshanks* the nickname ascribed to Edward I because of his long legs.
13 *braves* defiant insults.
    suffer tolerate.
14 *beard* defy with effrontery.
16 *magnanimity* courage, fortitude.
19 *counterbuffed of* opposed by.
20 *preach on poles* See 1.117 n.
22 *preachments* sermons.

EDWARD

    Yea, gentle Spencer, we have been too mild.

    Too kind to them, but now have drawn our sword,   25

    And if they send me not my Gaveston,

    We'll steel it on their crest and poll their tops.

BALDOCK

    This haught resolve becomes your majesty,

    Not to be tied to their affection

    As though your highness were a schoolboy still,   30

    And must be awed and governed like a child.

> *Enter* HUGH SPENCER [SENIOR] *an old man,*
> *father to the young* SPENCER [JUNIOR],
> *with his truncheon, and soldiers*

SPENCER SENIOR

    Long live my sovereign, the noble Edward,

    In peace triumphant, fortunate in wars.

EDWARD

    Welcome, old man. Com'st thou in Edward's aid?

    Then tell thy prince of whence and what thou art.   35

SPENCER SENIOR

    Lo, with a band of bowmen and of pikes,

    Brown bills and targeteers, four hundred strong,

    Sworn to defend King Edward's royal right,

    I come in person to your majesty:

    Spencer, the father of Hugh Spencer there,   40

    Bound to your highness everlastingly

    For favours done in him unto us all.

EDWARD

    Thy father, Spencer?

27   *steel it* i.e. sharpen his sword.
       poll their tops i.e. cut off their heads, punning on (i) the pollarding or cutting of tree-tops (ii) Spencer Junior's 'poles' (line 20 above).

28   *haught* haughty, lofty.

29   *affection* desire, will.

31   *awed* feared.

31   sd 3 *truncheon* staff that symbolized authority.

35   *of whence* from what place.
       what thou art i.e. what is your name.

36   *bowmen . . . pikes* Lances with sharp metal tips at both ends were driven into the ground just in front of the archers to protect them in battle.

37   *Brown bills* bronzed halberds (metonymic for the footsoldiers carrying them)
       targeteers shield-carrying infantrymen.

SPENCER JUNIOR

                 True, an it like your grace,
That pours in lieu of all your goodness shown,
His life, my lord, before your princely feet.   45

EDWARD

Welcome ten thousand times, old man, again.
Spencer, this love, this kindness to thy King
Argues thy noble mind and disposition.
Spencer, I here create thee Earl of Wiltshire,
And daily will enrich thee with our favour   50
That, as the sunshine, shall reflect o'er thee.
Beside, the more to manifest our love,
Because we hear Lord Bruce doth sell his land
And that the Mortimers are in hand withal,
Thou shalt have crowns of us, t'outbid the barons;   55
And Spencer, spare them not, but lay it on.
Soldiers, a largess, and thrice welcome all.

Enter [ISABELLA] *the Queen and* [PRINCE EDWARD]
her son, and LEVUNE, *a Frenchman*

SPENCER JUNIOR

My lord, here comes the Queen.

EDWARD   Madam, what news?

ISABELLA

News of dishonour, lord, and discontent:
Our friend Levune, faithful and full of trust,   60
Informeth us by letters and by words
That Lord Valois our brother, King of France,
Because your highness hath been slack in homage,
Hath seizèd Normandy into his hands.

---

43   *an it like* if it please.
47   For the first time, Edward addresses Spencer Senior by name; their relationship is
       now personal.
48   *Argues* proves. Ironically, this statement emphasizes the fact that Spencer Senior is
       not, by birth, a nobleman.
54   *in hand withal* i.e. engaged with this business.
56   *spare them not* i.e. do not be frugal (with the money).
       lay it on be extravagant, flamboyant.
57   *largess* liberal bestowal of money, bounty.
57   sd ed.; after line 58a in Q.
57   sd 2 ed. LEVUNE (*Lewne* Q; and throughout the text).
61   *words* oral report.

These be the letters, this the messenger. 65

EDWARD

Welcome Levune. [*To* ISABELLA] Tush, Sib, if this be all,
Valois and I will soon be friends again.
But to my Gaveston – shall I never see,
Never behold thee now? Madam, in this matter
We will employ you and your little son; 70
You shall go parley with the King of France.
Boy, see you bear you bravely to the King
And do your message with a majesty.

PRINCE EDWARD

Commit not to my youth things of more weight
Than fits a prince so young as I to bear. 75
And fear not, lord and father; heaven's great beams
On Atlas' shoulder shall not lie more safe
Than shall your charge committed to my trust.

ISABELLA

Ah, boy, this towardness makes thy mother fear
Thou art not marked to many days on earth. 80

EDWARD

Madam, we will that you with speed be shipped,
And this our son. Levune shall follow you
With all the haste we can dispatch him hence.
Choose of our lords to bear you company,
And go in peace; leave us in wars at home. 85

ISABELLA

Unnatural wars, where subjects brave their King:
God end them once. My lord, I take my leave
To make my preparation for France.
            [*Exeunt* ISABELLA, PRINCE EDWARD, *and* LEVUNE]

            Enter LORD MALTRAVERS

EDWARD

What, Lord Maltravers, dost thou come alone?

66   *Sib* 'affectionate diminutive of Isabella' (Gill).
77   *Atlas* In classical mythology, the Titan who carried the burden of the sky on his
       shoulders.
79   *towardness* boldness.
80   Ironically, King Edward III reigned for fifty years (1327–77).
87   *once* i.e. once and for all.

MALTRAVERS

    Yea, my good lord, for Gaveston is dead.   90

EDWARD

    Ah, traitors, have they put my friend to death?

    Tell me, Maltravers, died he ere thou cam'st,

    Or didst thou see my friend to take his death?

MALTRAVERS

    Neither, my lord, for as he was surprised,

    Begirt with weapons and with enemies round,   95

    I did your highness' message to them all,

    Demanding him of them – entreating rather –

    And said, upon the honour of my name.

    That I would undertake to carry him

    Unto your highness, and to bring him back.   100

EDWARD

    And tell me, would the rebels deny me that?

SPENCER JUNIOR

    Proud recreants!

EDWARD   Yea, Spencer, traitors all.

MALTRAVERS

    I found them at the first inexorable;

    The Earl of Warwick would not bide the hearing,

    Mortimer hardly; Pembroke and Lancaster   105

    Spake least. And when they flatly had denied,

    Refusing to receive me pledge for him,

    The Earl of Pembroke mildly thus bespake:

    'My lords, because our sovereign sends for him

    And promiseth he shall be safe returned,   110

    I will this undertake: to have him hence

    And see him re-delivered to your hands.'

EDWARD

    Well, and how fortunes that he came not?

SPENCER JUNIOR

    Some treason or some villainy was cause.

---

   94   *surprised* ambushed.

   95   *Begirt* encompassed, enclosed.

          round i.e. encircling, surrounding.

  102   *recreants* breakers of allegiance.

  104   *bide* endure, abide.

  113   *fortunes* chances.

MALTRAVERS

    The Earl of Warwick seized him on his way,   115

    For, being delivered unto Pembroke's men,

    Their lord rode home, thinking his prisoner safe;

    But ere he came, Warwick in ambush lay,

    And bare him to his death, and in a trench

    Struck off his head, and marched unto the camp.   120

SPENCER JUNIOR

    A bloody part, flatly against law of arms.

EDWARD

    O, shall I speak, or shall I sigh and die?

SPENCER JUNIOR

    My lord, refer your vengeance to the sword

    Upon these barons; hearten up your men.

    Let them not unrevenged murder your friends.   125

    Advance your standard, Edward, in the field,

    And march to fire them from their starting holes.

EDWARD [*Kneeling*]

    By earth, the common mother of us all,

    By heaven and all the moving orbs thereof,

    By this right hand and by my father's sword,   130

    And all the honours 'longing to my crown,

    I will have heads and lives for him as many

    As I have manors, castles, towns, and towers.

    Treacherous Warwick! Traitorous Mortimer!

    If I be England's king, in lakes of gore   135

    Your headless trunks, your bodies will I trail,

    That you may drink your fill and quaff in blood,

    And stain my royal standard with the same,

121   *part* action, deed.

       flatly absolutely.

123   *refer* assign.

126   *Advance your standard* Raise your ensign.

       in the field in battle.

127   *fire* smoke out.

       starting holes place of refuge for animals.

128   sd ed. (*Edward kneeles, and saith.* Q).

129   *moving orbs* In Ptolemaic cosmology, the moving concentric spheres surrounding the Earth; alternatively, the sun, moon, and planets, all of which were thought to orbit the Earth.

130   *father's sword* The sword was wielded by monarchs as a symbol of divine justice on Earth; cf. Romans 13:1–4.

131   *'longing* belonging

That so my bloody colours may suggest
Remembrance of revenge immortally 140
On your accursed traitorous progeny –
You villains that have slain my Gaveston.
And in this place of honour and of trust,
Spencer, sweet Spencer, I adopt thee here;
And merely of our love we do create thee 145
Earl of Gloucester and Lord Chamberlain,
Despite of times, despite of enemies.

SPENCER JUNIOR

My lord, here is a messenger from the barons
Desires access unto your majesty.

EDWARD

Admit him near 150

Enter the HERALD *from the Barons, with his coat of arms*

HERALD

Long live King Edward, England's lawful lord.

EDWARD

So wish not they, iwis, that sent thee hither.
Thou com'st from Mortimer and his complices –
A ranker rout of rebels never was.
Well, say thy message. 155

HERALD

The barons up in arms, by me salute
Your highness with long life and happiness,
And bid me say as plainer to your grace,
That if without effusion of blood
You will this grief have ease and remedy, 160
That from your princely person you remove
This Spencer, as a putrefying branch

---

141   *progeny* lineage.
145   *merely . . . love* i.e. rather than by right of succession; Spencer Junior was only a
        retainer of the previous Earl of Gloucester.
148   *here is* ed. (heres is Q1–2; heers Q3; heer's Q4).
151, 156 sp ed. HERALD (Q *Messen.*).
152   *iwis* assuredly.
153   *complices* confederates, conspirators.
154   *rout* (route Q; roote Q2–3; rout Q4); unruly crowd.
158   *plainer* complainant, one who brings an accusation.
159   *effusion* shedding (four syllables).

That deads the royal vine whose golden leaves
Impale your princely head, your diadem,
Whose brightness such pernicious upstarts dim,   165
Say they; and lovingly advise your grace
To cherish virtue and nobility,
And have old servitors in high esteem,
And shake off smooth dissembling flatterers.
This granted, they, their honours, and their lives   170
Are to your highness vowed and consecrate.

SPENCER JUNIOR

Ah, traitors, will they still display their pride?

EDWARD

Away! Tarry no answer, but be gone.
Rebels! Will they appoint their sovereign
His sports, his pleasures, and his company?   175
Yet ere thou go, see how I do divorce
Spencer from me.   *Embrace[s SPENCER JUNIOR]*
                 Now get thee to thy lords,
And tell them I will come to chastise them
For murdering Gaveston. Hie thee, get thee gone;
Edward with fire and sword follows at thy heels.   180
                                        [*Exit* HERALD]

My lords, perceive you how these rebels swell?
Soldiers, good hearts, defend your sovereign's right,
For now, even now, we march to make them stoop.
Away!
                                        Exeunt

163   *deads* deadens.
      royal vine Edward's crown was, in fact, decorated with four large and four small
      strawberry leaves. See *Boutell's Heraldry* (revised by J. P. Brooke-Little, London, 1970,
      p. 184).
164   *Impale* encircle.
      diadem crown.
168   *old servitors* retainers of long standing (Forker).
169   *smooth* (i) plausible (ii) obsequious.
171   *consecrate* made sacred.
173   *Tarry* wait for.
174   *appoint* order, grant
175   *sports* pastimes.
177   sd ed. (after 'deuorce' and 'lords,' respectively Q *Embrace / Spencer.*)
179   *Hie* hasten, hurry.
181   *lords* ed. (lord Q).
      swell grow proud.
183   *make them stoop* i.e. humiliate them.

[SCENE 12]

Alarums, excursions, a great fight, and a retreat

Enter [EDWARD] *the King*, SPENCER [SENIOR],
*s*PENCER JUNIOR, *and the noblemen of the King's side*

EDWARD
Why do we sound retreat? Upon them, lords!
This day I shall pour vengeance with my sword
On those proud rebels that are up in arms,
And do confront and countermand their King.
SPENCER JUNIOR
I doubt it not, my lord; right will prevail.   5
SPENCER SENIOR
'Tis not amiss, my liege, for either part
To breathe a while; our men with sweat and dust
All choked well near, begin to faint for heat,
And this retire refresheth horse and man.

Enter the barons, MORTIMER [JUNIOR], LANCASTER,
[KENT,] WARWICK, PEMBROKE, *with the others*

SPENCER JUNIOR
Here come the rebels.   10
MORTIMER JUNIOR
Look, Lancaster,
Yonder is Edward among his flatterers.
LANCASTER
And there let him be,
Till he pay dearly for their company.
WARWICK
And shall, or Warwick's sword shall smite in vain.   15

---

0   sd 1 *Alarums* battle-cries, trumpet signals.
         excursions rush of soldiers across the stage.
4   *countermand* oppose.
9   *retire* (i) respite (ii) retreat.
9   sd ed.; after line 10 in Q.
11–12   ed. (Looke ... his / flatterers. Q).
13–14   ed. (And ... for / their companie. Q).

EDWARD
What, rebels, do you shrink and sound retreat?
MORTIMER JUNIOR
No, Edward, no; thy flatterers faint and fly.
LANCASTER
Thou'd best betimes forsake thee and their trains,
For they'll betray thee, traitors as they are.
SPENCER JUNIOR
Traitor on thy face, rebellious Lancaster.   20
PEMBROKE
Away, base upstart; brav'st thou nobles thus?
SPENCER SENIOR
A noble attempt and honourable deed
Is it not, trow ye, to assemble aid
And levy arms against your lawful King?
EDWARD
For which ere long their heads shall satisfy   25
T'appease the wrath of their offended King.
MORTIMER JUNIOR
Then, Edward, thou wilt fight it to the last,
And rather bathe thy sword in subjects' blood
Than banish that pernicious company?
EDWARD
Ay, traitors all! Rather than thus be braved,   30
Make England's civil towns huge heaps of stones
And ploughs to go about our palace gates.
WARWICK
A desperate and unnatural resolution.
Alarum to the fight!
Saint George for England and the barons' right!   35
EDWARD
Saint George for England and King Edward's right!
                    [*Exeunt* WARWICK *with his men at one door
                    and* EDWARD *with his men at the other*]

18   *Thou'd* ed. (Th'ad Q) thou had.
      betimes in good time.
      trains tricks, political stratagems.
23   *trow* know, think.
25   *satisfy* atone, make amends.
34–5 ed. (Alarum ... England, / And ... right. Q).
35   *Saint George* Patron Saint of England (not adopted until Edward III's reign).

[SCENE 13]

> [*Alarums.*] *Enter* EDWARD, [SPENCER SENIOR,
> SPENCER JUNIOR, BALDOCK, LEVUNE, *and soldiers*]
> *with the Barons* [KENT, WARWICK, LANCASTER,
> *and* MORTIMER JUNIOR *and others*] *captives*

EDWARD

Now, lusty lords, now not by chance of war
But justice of the quarrel and the cause,
Vailed is your pride. Methinks you hang the heads,
But we'll advance them, traitors! Now 'tis time
To be avenged on you for all your braves   5
And for the murder of my dearest friend.
To whom right well you knew our soul was knit:
Good Piers of Gaveston, my sweet favourite –
Ah rebels, recreants, you made him away!

KENT

Brother, in regard of thee and of thy land,   10
Did they remove that flatterer from thy throne.

EDWARD

So, sir, you have spoke; away, avoid our presence.

> [*Exit* KENT]

Accursèd wretches, was't in regard of us,
When we had sent our messenger to request
He might be spared to come to speak with us,   15
And Pembroke undertook for his return,
That thou, proud Warwick, watched the prisoner,
Poor Piers, and headed him against law of arms?
For which thy head shall overlook the rest
As much as thou in rage outwent'st the rest.   20

---

0   sd 4 *and others* i.e. 'the rest' who are ordered to be executed at ll. 33–4.
3   *Vailed* lowered.
4   *advance* i.e. raise their severed heads on pikes.
5   *braves see* 11.13 n.
10   *in regard* out of consideration.
12   *avoid* depart from.
17   *watched* kept watch over.
18   *headed* beheaded.
19   *head . . . the rest* i.e. his severed head will be mounted higher than the others'.

WARWICK

    Tyrant, I scorn thy threats and menaces;

    'Tis but temporal that thou canst inflict.

LANCASTER

    The worst is death, and better die to live,

    Than live in infamy under such a king.

EDWARD

    Away with them, my lord of Winchester,   25

    These lusty leaders, Warwick and Lancaster.

    I charge you roundly off with both their heads.

    Away!

WARWICK

    Farewell, vain world.

LANCASTER   Sweet Mortimer, farewell.

         [*Exeunt* WARWICK *and* LANCASTER, *guarded by*

                               SPENCER SENIOR]

MORTIMER JUNIOR

    England, unkind to thy nobility,   30

    Groan for this grief; behold how thou art maimed.

EDWARD

    Go take that haughty Mortimer to the Tower;

    There see him safe bestowed. And for the rest.

    Do speedy execution on them all.

    Begone!   35

MORTIMER JUNIOR

    What, Mortimer! Can ragged stony walls

    Immure thy virtue that aspires to heaven?

    No, Edward, England's scourge, it may not be;

---

22   *but temporal* Edward can only inflict physical, not spiritual, suffering.

23   *The worst is death* Cf. *Richard II*, 'The worst is death, and death will have his day'
       (III.ii.99).

23–4   *better . . . infamy* proverbial (Tilley H 576).

25   *Winchester* Spencer Senior was created Earl of Wiltshire at 11.49, but is here
       addressed as Marquess of Winchester. In Marlowe's time, the two titles were held by
       the same person, William Paulet (*c.* 1532–98).

27   *roundly* without hesitation.

27–8   ed. (*one line in* Q).

29   *vain* worthless, futile.

34–5   ed. (*one line in* Q).

36   *ragged* rugged.

37   *Immure* enclose (within walls).   *virtue* power.

38   *scourge* often used by Marlowe to describe a ruler who lays waste a nation. Cf.
       2 Tamburlaine, 'Be all a scourge and terror to the world' (I.iii.63).

Mortimer's hope surmounts his fortune far.

                           [*Exit* MORTIMER JUNIOR *guarded*]

EDWARD

Sound drums and trumpets! March with me my friends;   40
Edward this day hath crowned him King anew.

                Exit[, *attended*], SPENCER [JUNIOR],
                    LEVUNE *and* BALDOCK *remain*

SPENCER JUNIOR

Levune, the trust that we repose in thee
Begets the quiet of King Edward's land.
Therefore be gone in haste, and with advice
Bestow that treasure on the lords of France;   45
That therewithal enchanted, like the guard
That suffered Jove to pass in showers of gold
To Danaë, all aid may be denied
To Isabel the Queen, that now in France
Makes friends, to cross the seas with her young son,   50
And step into his father's regiment.

LEVUNE

That's it these barons and the subtle Queen
Long levelled at.

BALDOCK   Yea, but Levune, thou seest
These barons lay their heads on blocks together;
What they intend, the hangman frustrates clean.   55

LEVUNE

Have you no doubts, my lords; I'll clap 's close
Among the lords of France with England's gold
That Isabel shall make her plaints in vain,
And France shall be obdurate with her tears.

39   *surmounts* surpasses, rises above.
41   sd ed. (*Manent Spencer filius, Lewne & Baldock.* Q).
42   *repose* place.
43   *Begets* will produce, obtain.
46   *therewithal* ed. (therewith all Q).
46–8 *like . . . Danaë* See 6.53 n.
51   *regiment* rule, authority.
52   *subtle* cunning, insidious.
53   *levelled at* ed. (leuied at Q) aimed at.
55   *clean* completely, absolutely.
56   *clap 's* ed. (claps Q); 'clap us'; strike a bargain. Clap usually referred to the clapping
      of hands when securing a transaction.
      close secretly.
59   *obdurate* unyielding.

SPENCER JUNIOR
    Then make for France amain; Levune, away!   60
    Proclaim King Edward's wars and victories.

Exeunt

[SCENE 14]

Enter EDMUND [*the* EARL OF KENT]

KENT
    Fair blows the wind for France; blow, gentle gale,
    Till Edmund be arrived for England's good.
    Nature, yield to my country's cause in this:
    A brother – no, a butcher of thy friends –
    Proud Edward, dost thou banish me thy presence?   5
    But I'll to France, and cheer the wrongèd Queen,
    And certify what Edward's looseness is.
    Unnatural King, to slaughter noblemen
    And cherish flatterers. Mortimer, I stay
    Thy sweet escape; stand gracious, gloomy night   10
    To his device.

Enter MORTIMER [JUNIOR] *disguised*

MORTIMER JUNIOR
    Holla! Who walketh there? Is't you my lord?
KENT
    Mortimer, 'tis I;
    But hath thy potion wrought so happily?
MORTIMER JUNIOR
    It hath, my lord; the warders all asleep,   15

---

60   *amain* at once.

1   *gentle* not stormy, but also implying courtesy or generosity.
7   *looseness* (i) carelessness, incompetence (ii) sexual misconduct.
9   *stay* await.
10–11   Kent invokes the darkness of night to aid Mortimer Junior's escape.
11   *device* stratagem, intent.
13–14   ed. (*Mortimer . . .* so / happilie? Q).
14   *thy potion . . . happily?* i.e. have the guards been successfully drugged?

I thank them, gave me leave to pass in peace.
But hath your grace got shipping unto France?
KENT

Fear it not.

Exeunt

[SCENE 15]

Enter [ISABELLA] *the Queen and her son* [PRINCE EDWARD]

ISABELLA

Ah boy, our friends do fail us all in France;
The lords are cruel and the King unkind.
What shall we do?
PRINCE EDWARD   Madam, return to England
And please my father well, and then a fig
For all my uncle's friendship here in France.   5
I warrant you, I'll win his highness quickly;
A loves me better than a thousand Spencers.
ISABELLA

Ah boy, thou art deceived at least in this,
To think that we can yet be tuned together.
No, no, we jar too far. Unkind Valois!   10
Unhappy Isabel! When France rejects,
Whither, O whither dost thou bend thy steps?

Enter SIR JOHN OF HAINAULT

16   *gave me leave* allowed me.

4   *a fig* obscene expression of contempt; usually accompanied by a phallic gesture in which the thumb was thrust into the mouth or between two closed fingers. Proverbial (Tilley F 210).

6   *warrant* assure.
7   *A* unstressed form of 'he'.
9   *yet* still.
10   *jar* (i) become discordant, playing upon the metaphor of the previous line (ii) quarrel.
11   *Unhappy* unfortunate, unlucky.
12   *bend . . . steps* i.e. what course of action should I next take?

SIR JOHN
    Madam, what cheer?
ISABELLA   Ah, good Sir John of Hainault,
    Never so cheerless, nor so far distressed.
SIR JOHN
    I hear, sweet lady, of the King's unkindness.   15
    But droop not, madam; noble minds contemn
    Despair. Will your grace with me to Hainault
    And there stay time's advantage with your son?
    How say you, my lord, will you go with your friends,
    And shake off all our fortunes equally?   20
PRINCE EDWARD
    So pleaseth the Queen, my mother, me it likes.
    The King of England nor the court of France
    Shall have me from my gracious mother's side,
    Till I be strong enough to break a staff,
    And then have at the proudest Spencer's head.   25
SIR JOHN
    Well said, my lord.
ISABELLA
    Oh, my sweet heart, how do I moan thy wrongs.
    Yet triumph in the hope of thee, my joy.
    Ah, sweet Sir John, even to the utmost verge
    Of Europe, or the shore of Tanais,   30
    Will we with thee to Hainault, so we will.
    The Marquis is a noble gentleman;
    His grace, I dare presume, will welcome me.

              Enter EDMUND [*the* EARL OF KENT]
                 and MORTIMER [JUNIOR]

13   *what cheer* i.e. what is your mood, disposition?
16   *contemn* despise, disregard.
17   *Hainault* Flemish county in the Low Countries, bordering France.
20   *shake off* cast off.
21   *So* as it.
24   *staff a* lance or quarter-staff, used (and broken) in combat.
25   *have at* attack, strike at (imperative).
27   *moan* lament (aloud).
29   *utmost verge* i.e. the furthest limit.
30   *Tanais* the Latin name for the River Don which the Elizabethans regarded as the
       boundary between Europe and Asia.
32   *Marquis* i.e. Sir John's brother, William, Count of Hainault.
33   sd ed.; after line 34a in Q.

But who are these?

KENT   Madam, long may you live
Much happier than your friends in England do.   35

ISABELLA
Lord Edmund and Lord Mortimer alive!
Welcome to France. The news was here, my lord,
That you were dead, or very near your death.

MORTIMER JUNIOR
Lady, the last was truest of the twain;
But Mortimer, reserved for better hap,   40
Hath shaken off the thraldom of the Tower,
[*To* PRINCE EDWARD]
And lives t'advance your standard, good my lord.

PRINCE EDWARD
How mean you, an the King my father lives?
No, my lord Mortimer, not I, I trow.

ISABELLA
Not, son? Why not? I would it were no worse;   45
But gentle lords, friendless we are in France.

MORTIMER JUNIOR
Monsieur le Grand, a noble friend of yours,
Told us at our arrival all the news:
How hard the nobles, how unkind the King
Hath showed himself. But madam, right makes room   50
Where weapons want; and though a many friends
Are made away – as Warwick, Lancaster,
And others of our party and faction –
Yet have we friends, assure your grace, in England
Would cast up caps and clap their hands for joy,   55
To see us there appointed for our foes.

40   *hap* fortune.
41   *thraldom* servitude, bondage.
42   *t'advance your standard* i.e. raise the banner or ensign of battle.
44   *trow* think, reckon.
47   *Monsieur le Grand* an invented character with no historical original.
49   *hard* difficult, obdurate.
        unkind unnatural (to his sister, Isabella).
        the King i.e. the King of France.
50   *makes room* makes way.
51   *want* i.e. are required. *a many* many.
52   *made away* i.e. dead (implicitly by murder and treachery).
55   *cast up caps* i.e. throw caps into the air as a sign of joy.
56   *appointed* armed, prepared for battle.

KENT

    Would all were well and Edward well reclaimed,

    For England's honour, peace, and quietness.

MORTIMER JUNIOR

    But by the sword, my lord, it must be deserved.

    The King will ne'er forsake his flatterers.   60

SIR JOHN

    My lords of England, sith the ungentle King

    Of France refuseth to give aid of arms

    To this distressèd queen his sister here,

    Go you with her to Hainault. Doubt ye not,

    We will find comfort, money, men, and friends   65

    Ere long, to bid the English King a base.

    How say, young prince, what think you of the match?

PRINCE EDWARD

    I think King Edward will outrun us all.

ISABELLA

    Nay son, not so; and you must not discourage

    Your friends that are so forward in your aid.   70

KENT

    Sir John of Hainault, pardon us, I pray;

    These comforts that you give our woeful Queen

    Bind us in kindness all at your command.

ISABELLA

    Yea, gentle brother; and the God of heaven

    Prosper your happy motion, good Sir John.   75

MORTIMER JUNIOR

    This noble gentleman, forward in arms,

    Was born, I see, to be our anchor-hold.

    Sir John of Hainault, be it thy renown

    That England's Queen and nobles in distress

    Have been by thee restored and comforted.   80

---

57   *reclaimed* subdued.

59   *deserved* earned.

61   *sith* since.

66   *bid . . . a base* challenge to risk capture (from 'prisoner's base', a children's game involving running between two 'bases', between which the players might be caught by their opponents).

67   *match* game.

74   *brother* i.e. brother-in-law.

75   *motion* proposal.

76   *forward* ardent.

SIR JOHN

    Madam, along, and you, my lord, with me,
    That England's peers may Hainault's welcome see.

                                          [*Exeunt*]

[SCENE 16]

Enter [EDWARD] *the King,* MALTRAVERS, *the two* SPENCERS,
[SENIOR *and* JUNIOR,] *with others*

EDWARD

    Thus after many threats of wrathful war,
    Triumpheth England's Edward with his friends;
    And triumph Edward with his friends uncontrolled.
    [*To* SPENCER JUNIOR]
    My lord of Gloucester, do you hear the news?

SPENCER JUNIOR

    What news, my lord?   5

EDWARD

    Why man, they say there is great execution
    Done through the realm. My lord of Arundel,
    You have the note, have you not?

MALTRAVERS

    From the Lieutenant of the Tower, my lord.

EDWARD

    I pray let us see it. What have we there?   10
    Read it Spencer.

                SPENCER [JUNIOR] *reads their names*

---

   3   *uncontrolled* without censure.
   8   *note* official list.
 11   sd SPENCER [JUNIOR] *reads their names* The details of those who have been executed
        are not included in the control text, thus creating some staging difficulties. Holin-
        shed supplies the list reproduced in the ruled box on p. 89; if required, this might
        be interpolated in performance.

> ## Extract from Holinshed,
> ### *Chronicles of England, Scotland, and Ireland*
> ## (1587 edn, vol. 3, p. 331)
>
> ... the Lord William Tuchet, the Lord William Fitzwilliam, the
> Lord Warren de Lisle, the Lord Henry Bradborne, and the Lord
> William Chenie, barons, with John Page, an esquire, were drawn
> and hanged at Pomfret ... and then shortly after, Roger Lord
> Clifford, John Lord Mowbray, and Sir Gosein D'Eivill, barons,   5
> were drawn and hanged at York. At Bristol in like manner were
> executed Sir Henry de Willington and Sir Henry Montfort,
> baronets; and at Gloucester, the Lord John Gifford and Sir
> William Elmebridge, knight; and at London, the Lord Henry
> Tyes, baron; at Winchelsea, Sir Thomas Culpepper, knight; at   10
> Windsor, the Lord Francis de Aldham, baron; and at Canterbury,
> the Lord Bartholomew de Badlesmere and the Lord Bartho-
> lomew de Ashburnham, barons. Also, at Cardiff in Wales, Sir
> William Fleming, knight, was executed. Divers were executed in
> their counties, as Sir Thomas Mandit and others.   15
>
> 4 *Pomfret* Pontefract
> 15 *counties* ed. (Holinshed reads countries)

Why so, they 'barked apace a month ago;
Now, on my life, they'll neither bark nor bite.
Now, sirs, the news from France; Gloucester, I trow
The lords of France love England's gold so well   15
As Isabella gets no aid from thence.
What now remains? Have you proclaimed, my lord,
Reward for them can bring in Mortimer?

SPENCER JUNIOR
My lord, we have; and if he be in England,
A will be had ere long, I doubt it not.   20

12   *'barked* embarked on committing treason (Forker).
      apace swiftly.
13   *neither bark nor bite* Edward puns on the previous line, introducing a proverbial
      meaning (Tilley B 85, B 86).
15   *love England's gold* i.e. Edward's bribe has worked.
16   *Isabella* ed. (*Isabell* Q).
20   *A* he, i.e. Mortimer Junior.
      had captured (Forker).

EDWARD

If, dost thou say? Spencer, as true as death,
He is in England's ground; our port masters
Are not so careless of their King's command.

Enter a POST [*with letters*]

How now, what news with thee? From whence come these?

POST

Letters, my lord, and tidings forth of France   25
To you, my lord of Gloucester, from Levune.

EDWARD

Read.

SPENCER JUNIOR (*Reads the letter*)

'My duty to your honour premised, *et cetera*, I have according
to instructions in that behalf, dealt with the King of France's
lords, and effected, that the Queen, all discontented and dis-   30
comforted, is gone. Whither? If you ask, with Sir John of
Hainault, brother to the Marquis, into Flanders. With them are
gone Lord Edmund and the Lord Mortimer, having in their
company divers of your nation, and others; and, as constant report goeth, they intend to give King Edward battle in   35
England sooner than he can look for them. This is all the news
of import.

Your honour's in all service, Levune.'

EDWARD

Ah, villains, hath that Mortimer escaped?
With him is Edmund gone associate?   40
And will Sir John of Hainault lead the round?
Welcome, i' God's name, madam, and your son;

---

21   *as true as death* proverbial (Tilley D 136).
27–8 ed. (Reade. / *Spencer reades the letter.* Q).
28   *premised* ed. (promised Q; premised Q2); that which serves as a formal prefix or
      introduction to a report.
      et cetera ed. (&c. Q).
28–9 *according . . . in that behalf* i.e. with respect to Edward's instructions.
29   *France's* ed. (Fraunce his Q).
30   *effected* i.e. have caused, brought about.
30–1 *discomforted* discouraged.
34–5 *constant* consistent, reliable.
35–6 *they intend . . . for them* i.e. they will take the initiative in challenging Edward to
      fight before he is ready.
37   *import* importance.
41   *round* dance.

England shall welcome you and all your rout.
Gallop apace bright Phoebus through the sky,
And dusky night, in rusty iron car,   45
Between you both shorten the time, I pray,
That I may see that most desired day
When we may meet these traitors in the field.
Ah, nothing grieves me but my little boy,
Is thus misled to countenance their ills,   50
Come, friends, to Bristol, there to make us strong;
And, winds, as equal be to bring them in
As you injurious were to bear them forth.

                                                        [*Exeunt*]

[SCENE 17]

Enter [ISABELLA] *the Queen, her son* [PRINCE EDWARD],
EDMUND [*the* EARL OF KENT], MORTIMER [JUNIOR],
and SIR JOHN [OF HAINAULT, *with soldiers*]

ISABELLA
Now lords, our loving friends and countrymen,
Welcome to England all. With prosperous winds
Our kindest friends in Belgia have we left,
To cope with friends at home. A heavy case,
When force to force is knit, and sword and glaive   5

43   *rout* unruly followers.
44   *Phoebus* Phoebus Apollo, the sun god of classical mythology, who drove the sun
       across the sky in a chariot.
45   *dusky night . . . car* Cf. *1 Tamburlaine*, 'ugly Darkness with her rusty coach' (V.i.294).
50   *countenance* favour, support.
       ills sins, wickedness.
51   *strong* resolute, determined.
52   *equal* just.

2   *prosperous* favourable.
3   *Belgia* the Low Countries.
4   *cope* engage in battle.
       friends kinsfolk, relatives.
       heavy case sad predicament.
5   *glaive* variously used of the spear, halberd, and broadsword.

In civil broils makes kin and countrymen
Slaughter themselves in others, and their sides
With their own weapons gored. But what's the help?
Misgoverned kings are cause of all this wrack;
And Edward, thou art one among them all,   10
Whose looseness hath betrayed thy land to spoil
And made the channels overflow with blood.
Of thine own people patron shouldst thou be,
But thou –

MORTIMER JUNIOR
                    Nay madam, if you be a warrior,
Ye must not grow so passionate in speeches.   15
Lords, sith that we are by sufferance of heaven
Arrived and armèd in this prince's right,
Here for our country's cause swear we to him
All homage, fealty, and forwardness.
And for the open wrongs and injuries   20
Edward hath done to us, his Queen, and land,
We come in arms to wreak it with the sword,
That England's Queen in peace may repossess
Her dignities and honours, and withal
We may remove these flatterers from the King,   25
That havocs England's wealth and treasury.

SIR JOHN
Sound trumpets, my lord, and forward let us march;
Edward will think we come to flatter him.

KENT
I would he never had been flattered more.

                    [*Sound trumpets. Exeunt*]

---

6   *civil broils* i.e. civil wars.
8   *help* remedy.
9   *Misgoverned* unruly.
        wrack destruction.
11   *looseness* (i) frivolous, careless behaviour (ii) lasciviousness.
13–14a ed. (*one line in* Q).
13   *patron* father-figure (and hence an example).
16   *sufferance* permission.
19   *fealty* loyalty, fidelity.   *forwardness* eagerness.
22   *wreak* ed. (wrecke Q: a variant form of wreak) avenge.
        sword ed. (swords Q; sworde Q2–3; sword Q4).
26   *havocs . . . treasury* i.e. misuses (literally lays waste) public money by indiscriminate
        spending.

[SCENE 18]

Enter [EDWARD] *the King*, BALDOCK,
and SPENCER [JUNIOR], *flying about the stage*

SPENCER JUNIOR
> Fly, fly, my lord! The Queen is over-strong;
> Her friends do multiply and yours do fail.
> Shape we our course to Ireland, there to breathe.

EDWARD
> What, was I born to fly and run away,
> And leave the Mortimers conquerors behind?   5
> Give me my horse, and let's r'enforce our troops.
> And in this bed of honour die with fame.

BALDOCK
> O no, my lord; this princely resolution
> Fits not the time. Away! We are pursued.

> > > > > > > > > > > > > > > > [*Exeunt*]

[Enter] EDMUND [*the* EARL OF KENT]
alone with a sword and target

KENT
> This way he fled, but I am come too late   10
> Edward, alas, my heart relents for thee.
> Proud traitor Mortimer, why dost thou chase
> Thy lawful King, thy sovereign, with thy sword?
> Vile wretch, and why hast thou of all unkind,
> Borne arms against thy brother and thy King?   15
> Rain showers of vengeance on my cursèd head,
> Thou God, to whom in justice it belongs

---

1   *Fly* run.
2   *multiply* increase.
     fail (i) become exhausted (ii) fall, die (iii) decline in number.
3   *Shape* steer.
5   *the Mortimers* Gill notes that the historical Mortimer Senior was, at this point, already dead.
6   *r'enforce* urge, encourage (once more).
7   *bed of honour* i.e. England.
9   sd 2 *target* lightweight shield.
14   *Vile wretch* Kent addresses himself.
     unkind unnatural (because he has acted against his own brother).

To punish this unnatural revolt.
Edward, this Mortimer aims at thy life;
O fly him then! But Edmund, calm this rage; 20
Dissemble or thou diest, for Mortimer
And Isabel do kiss while they conspire;
And yet she bears a face of love, forsooth.
Fie on that love that hatcheth death and hate!
Edmund, away; Bristol to Longshanks' blood 25
Is false. Be not found single for suspect;
Proud Mortimer pries near into thy walks.

Enter [ISABELLA] *the Queen,* MORTIMER [JUNIOR],
the young PRINCE [EDWARD], *and* SIR JOHN OF HAINAULT

ISABELLA

Successful battles gives the God of kings
To them that fight in right and fear his wrath.
Since then successfully we have prevailed, 30
Thanks be heaven's great architect and you.
Ere farther we proceed, my noble lords,
We here create our well-beloved son,
Of love and care unto his royal person,
Lord Warden of the realm; and sith the fates 35
Have made his father so infortunate,
Deal you, my lords, in this, my loving lords,
As to your wisdoms fittest seems in all.

KENT

Madam, without offence, if I may ask,
How will you deal with Edward in his fall? 40

---

19   *aims . . . life* i.e. intends to kill you.
21   *Dissemble* i.e. be a hypocrite, be deceptive.
23   *forsooth* certainly, in truth (said with irony and contempt).
25–6   *Bristol . . . false* i.e. the Mayor of Bristol has betrayed the son of King Edward I (cf.
        11.12 n.).
26   *single* alone, by oneself.
        for suspect i.e. for this causes suspicion.
27   *walks* movements.
31   *you* i.e. Isabella's allies.
34   *Of* out of.
35   *Lord Warden* viceroy, usually appointed during a king's minority or absence.
        fates goddesses of destiny.
36   *infortunate* unfortunate.
37   *Deal* act, proceed.
38   *fittest* most suitable, agreeable.

PRINCE EDWARD

Tell me, good uncle, what Edward do you mean?

KENT

Nephew, your father; I dare not call him King.

MORTIMER JUNIOR

My lord of Kent, what needs these questions?

'Tis not in her controlment, nor in ours,

But as the realm and Parliament shall please,   45

So shall your brother be disposed of.

[*Aside to* ISABELLA] I like not this relenting mood in Edmund;

Madam, 'tis good to look to him betimes.

ISABELLA [*Aside to* MORTIMER JUNIOR]

My lord, the Mayor of Bristol knows our mind?

MORTIMER JUNIOR [*Aside*]

Yea, madam, and they 'scape not easily   50

That fled the field.

ISABELLA   Baldock is with the King;

A goodly chancellor, is he not, my lord?

SIR JOHN

So are the Spencers, the father and the son.

KENT [*To himself*]

This Edward is the ruin of the realm.

> *Enter* RHYS AP HOWELL, *and the* MAYOR OF BRISTOL,
> *with* SPENCER [SENIOR, *guarded by soldiers*]

RHYS AP HOWELL

God save Queen Isabel and her princely son.   55

Madam, the Mayor and citizens of Bristol,

In sign of love and duty to this presence,

Present by me this traitor to the state –

Spencer, the father to that wanton Spencer,

That, like the lawless Catiline of Rome,   60

Revelled in England's wealth and treasury.

41 'Kent is ungently reproved for lack of respect (by not referring to Edward by his title)' (Gill).
44 *controlment* (i) power (ii) ability to restrain.
47 *relenting* pitying.
48 *look to him* i.e. in anticipation of a change of loyalties.
    betimes in good time.
49 *knows our mind* i.e. is acquainted with our intentions.
57 *presence* i.e. royal presence.
60 *Catiline* Lucius Sergius Catalina (d. 62 BC), a corrupt Roman nobleman who was a byword for treason in the 1590s.

ISABELLA

We thank you all.

MORTIMER JUNIOR Your loving care in this

Deserveth princely favours and rewards.

But where's the King and the other Spencer fled?

RHYS AP HOWELL

Spencer the son, created Earl of Gloucester, 65

Is with that smooth-tongued scholar Baldock gone,

And shipped but late for Ireland with the King.

MORTIMER JUNIOR

Some whirlwind fetch them back, or sink them all!

They shall be started thence, I doubt it not.

PRINCE EDWARD

Shall I not see the King my father yet? 70

KENT [Aside]

Unhappy Edward, chased from England's bounds.

SIR JOHN

Madam, what resteth? Why stand ye in a muse?

ISABELLA

I rue my lord's ill fortune, but, alas,

Care of my country called me to this war.

MORTIMER JUNIOR

Madam, have done with care and sad complaint; 75

Your King hath wronged your country and himself,

And we must seek to right it as we may.

Meanwhile, have hence this rebel to the block;

Your lordship cannot privilege your head.

SPENCER SENIOR

Rebel is he that fights against his prince; 80

So fought not they that fought in Edward's right.

MORTIMER JUNIOR

Take him away; he prates.

[Exit SPENCER SENIOR, guarded]

67   *but late* just lately.
69   *started* forced out (as an animal driven from its hiding-place).
71   *Unhappy* ed. (Vnhappies Q).
      bounds territory.
72   *resteth* remains to be done.
      in a muse in thought, perplexed.
78   *have hence* take away.
79   Spencer Senior's newly acquired status saves him from hanging, but not decapitation.
80   *prince* ruler.

You, Rhys ap Howell,
. Shall do good service to her majesty,
Being of countenance in your country here,
To follow these rebellious runagates. 85
We in meanwhile, madam, must take advice
How Baldock, Spencer, and their complices
May in their fall be followed to their end.

Exeunt

[SCENE 19]

Enter the ABBOT, MONKS, [*King*] EDWARD,
SPENCER [JUNIOR], *and* BALDOCK[, *the
latter three disguised as clergy*]

ABBOT

Have you no doubt, my lord, have you no fear;
As silent and as careful will we be
To keep your royal person safe with us.
Free from suspect and fell invasion
Of such as have your majesty in chase – 5
Yourself, and those your chosen company –
As danger of this stormy time requires.

EDWARD

Father, thy face should harbour no deceit;
O hadst thou ever been a king, thy heart,
Pierced deeply with sense of my distress, 10
Could not but take compassion of my state.
Stately and proud, in riches and in train,

---

84   *countenance* authority, influence.
85   *runagates* (i) renegades (ii) traitors. In Elizabethan England the term was associated
         with voluntary Catholic exiles who were, it was thought, trained for sedition and
         assassination in the continental seminaries.
86   *must take advice* i.e. consider, deliberate.
87   *complices* accomplices.
88   *followed to their end* i.e. pursued to their deaths.

4   *suspect* suspicion.
      fell cruel.
5   *in chase* i.e. being pursued, hunted (like an animal in sport).

Whilom I was powerful and full of pomp;
But what is he, whom rule and empery
Have not in life or death made miserable?   15
Come Spencer, come Baldock, come sit down by me;
Make trial now of that philosophy
That in our famous nurseries of arts
Thou sucked'st from Plato and from Aristotle.
Father, this life contemplative is heaven –   20
O that I might this life in quiet lead!
But we, alas, are chased; and you, my friends,
Your lives and my dishonour they pursue.
Yet, gentle monks, for treasure, gold nor fee,
Do you betray us and our company.   25

MONKS

Your grace may sit secure, if none but we
Do wot of your abode.

SPENCER JUNIOR

Not one alive; but shrewdly I suspect
A gloomy fellow in a mead below;
A gave a long look after us, my lord,   30
And all the land, I know, is up in arms –
Arms that pursue our lives with deadly hate.

BALDOCK

We were embarked for Ireland, wretched we,
With awkward winds and sore tempests driven
To fall on shore and here to pine in fear   35

13   *Whilom* formerly.
      pomp splendour, magnificence.
14   *empery* dominion.
18   *nurseries of arts* i.e. the universities of Oxford and Cambridge.
20   *life contemplative* The 'contemplative life', as distinct from the 'active life' (both
      concepts derived from St Augustine's *City of God*), entailed religious devotion and
      solitude.
27   *wot* know.
28   *shrewdly* intuitively.
29   *gloomy fellow* the Mower, whom Spencer Junior supposes to be the figure of Death
      the Grim Reaper in the field, holding a scythe. While this 'vision' adds to the tragic
      sense of foreboding, it may also suggest that Spencer Junior's imagination is being
      affected by exhaustion or fear.
      mead meadow.
      below i.e. down, outside the abbey.
34   *sore* harsh.
35   *fall on shore* become grounded.

Of Mortimer and his confederates.

EDWARD

Mortimer! Who talks of Mortimer?
Who wounds me with the name of Mortimer,
That bloody man? [*He kneels*] Good father, on thy lap
Lay I this head, laden with mickle care.   40
O might I never open these eyes again,
Never again lift up this drooping head,
O never more lift up this dying heart!

SPENCER JUNIOR

Look up, my lord. Baldock, this drowsiness
Betides no good. Here even we are betrayed.   45

> *Enter, with Welsh hooks,* RHYS AP HOWELL, *a* MOWER,
> *and the* EARL OF LEICESTER[, *with soldiers*]

MOWER

Upon my life, those be the men ye seek.

RHYS AP HOWELL

Fellow, enough. [*To* LEICESTER] My lord, I pray be short;
A fair commission warrants what we do.

LEICESTER [*Aside*]

The Queen's commission, urged by Mortimer.
What cannot gallant Mortimer with the Queen?   50
Alas, see where he sits and hopes unseen
T'escape their hands that seek to reave his life.
Too true it is: *quem dies vidit veniens superbum,*
Hunc dies vidit fugiens iacentem.
But Leicester, leave to grow so passionate.   55

---

39   *bloody* bloodthirsty, causing bloodshed.
40   *mickle* much.
44   *drowsiness* traditionally an ill omen.
45   *Betides* bodes.
45   sd 1 *Welsh hooks* scythe-like tools. Michael J. Warren convincingly argues that these
      are long-handled hedging-bills and not, as many editors have previously assumed,
      military weapons. This would make sense considering the presence of the Mower.
      See 'Welsh Hooks in *Edward II*', *N&Q*, n.s. 25 (1978), 109–10.
48   *fair commission* formal written authority.
      warrants authorizes.
50   *gallant* (i) bold (ii) lover.
52   *reave* take away by force.
53–4 *quem dies ... iacentem* taken from Seneca's *Thyestes*, ll. 613–14. Translated by Jasper
      Heywood in 1560: 'Whom dawne of day hath seene in pryde to raygne, / Hym
      overthrowne hath seene the evening late.'

[*Aloud*] Spencer and Baldock, by no other names,
I arrest you of high treason here.
Stand not on tides, but obey th'arrest;
'Tis in the name of Isabel the Queen.
My lord, why droop you thus?   60

EDWARD

O day! The last of all my bliss on earth,
Centre of all misfortune. O my stars!
Why do you lour unkindly on a king?
Comes Leicester, then, in Isabella's name
To take my life, my company, from me?   65
Here, man, rip up this panting breast of mine
And take my heart in rescue of my friends.

RHYS AP HOWELL

Away with them.

SPENCER JUNIOR   It may become thee yet
To let us take our farewell of his grace.

ABBOT

My heart with pity earns to see this sight;   70
A king to bear these words and proud commands!

EDWARD

Spencer, ah sweet Spencer, thus then must we part?

SPENCER JUNIOR

We must, my lord; so will the angry heavens.

EDWARD

Nay, so will hell and cruel Mortimer;
The gentle heavens have not to do in this.   75

BALDOCK

My lord, it is in vain to grieve or storm.
Here humbly of your grace we take our leaves;
Our lots are cast. I fear me, so is thine.

---

56   *no other names* Spencer Junior and Baldock are stripped of their recently acquired
        titles ('names').
58   *Stand* (i) assert (ii) rely on. The favourites are warned that they cannot expect the
        protection of noble privileges.
61–2   Cf. 10.4–5.
63   *lour* frown, look angry.
66   *panting* (of the heart) palpitating.
67   *rescue* release from legal custody.
70   *earns* grieves.
73, 74 *will* command, determine.
76   *storm* make a commotion.

EDWARD

In heaven we may, in earth never shall we meet.
And Leicester, say, what shall become of us?   80

LEICESTER

Your majesty must go to Kenilworth.

EDWARD

'Must'! 'Tis somewhat hard when kings must go.

LEICESTER

Here is a litter ready for your grace
That waits your pleasure; and the day grows old.

RHYS AP HOWELL

As good be gone, as stay and be benighted.   85

EDWARD

A litter hast thou? Lay me in a hearse,
And to the gates of hell convey me hence;
Let Pluto's bells ring out my fatal knell,
And hags howl for my death at Charon's shore,
For friends hath Edward none but these, and these,   90
And these must die under a tyrant's sword.

RHYS AP HOWELL

My lord, be going; care not for these,
For we shall see them shorter by the heads.

EDWARD

Well, that shall be shall be; part we must:
Sweet Spencer, gentle Baldock, part we must.   95
Hence feignèd weeds, unfeignèd are my woes.
Father, farewell. Leicester, thou stay'st for me.
And go I must. Life, farewell with my friends.

81   *Kenilworth* Q's old-spelling form, 'Killingworth', has an ominous aptness; some
      productions may wish to retain it in preference to the modernized version. See the
      Note on the Text for a full discussion of the modernization.

83   *litter* coach for one person which was usually carried by two men.

85   i.e. it would be best to leave for Kenilworth before nightfall.

88   *Pluto's bells* In classical mythology, Pluto was the keeper of the underworld and ruler
      of the dead. The bells were not part of classical tradition but probably represent the
      death knell ringing out for those about to die.

89   *Charon* the ferryman of the classical underworld who transported the dead across
      the River Styx.

90   *but these . . . these* This could be an implicit stage direction prompting Edward to
      gesticulate or point to Spencer Junior and Baldock.

93   i.e. they will be beheaded.

96   *feignèd* false.
      weeds clothes. Cf. Peele's *Edward I*, 'Hence faigned weedes, unfeigned is my griefe'
      (2519).

Exeunt EDWARD *and* LEICESTER

SPENCER JUNIOR

O, is he gone? Is noble Edward gone,
Parted from hence, never to see us more?   100
Rend, sphere of heaven, and fire forsake thy orb!
Earth melt to air! Gone is my sovereign,
Gone, gone, alas, never to make return.

BALDOCK

Spencer, I see our souls are fleeted hence;
We are deprived the sunshine of our life.   105
Make for a new life, man; throw up thy eyes,
And heart and hand to heaven's immortal throne,
Pay nature's debt with cheerful countenance.
Reduce we all our lessons unto this:
To die, sweet Spencer, therefore live we all;   110
Spencer, all live to die, and rise to fall.

RHYS AP HOWELL

Come, come, keep these preachments till you come to the place
appointed. You, and such as you are, have made wise work in
England. Will your lordships away?

MOWER

Your worship, I trust, will remember me?   115

RHYS AP HOWELL

Remember thee, fellow? What else?
Follow me to the town.

[*Exeunt*]

---

101 *Rend* ed. (Rent Q) be torn apart.
     sphere of heaven the Sun.
104 *fleeted hence* i.e. have flown out of the body.
105 *sunshine of our life* The king was frequently likened to the sun in Elizabethan drama.
     Cf. Shakespeare, *Richard II*, III.iii.61–2.
108 *Pay nature's debt* i.e. die; proverbial (Tilley D 168).
109 *Reduce* summarize.
     lessons learning. Ironically, Baldock's last words recall his earlier scholastic preten-
     sions.
110–11 Baldock resigns himself to death by reflecting that we are born to die; but his medita-
     tion also invokes the medieval 'de casibus' notion of tragedy in which an individual's
     rise to success is always followed by their fall.
112–14 ed. (Come . . . till / you . . . appointed / You . . . in / England. / Will . . . away? Q).
112 *preachments* sermons.
112–13 *place appointed* i.e. the scaffold.
113 *made . . . work* created havoc, caused trouble.
115 i.e. will you reward me?
116 *What else?* But of course!

[SCENE 20]

Enter [EDWARD] *the King,* LEICESTER, *with
the* BISHOP [OF WINCHESTER, *and* TRUSSEL]
for the crown[, *and attendants*]

LEICESTER

Be patient, good my lord, cease to lament.
Imagine Kenilworth Castle were your court.
And that you lay for pleasure here a space,
Not of compulsion or necessity.

EDWARD

Leicester, if gentle words might comfort me,   5
Thy speeches long ago had eased my sorrows,
For kind and loving hast thou always been.
The griefs of private men are soon allayed,
But not of kings: the forest deer, being struck,
Runs to an herb that closeth up the wounds;   10
But when the imperial lion's flesh is gored,
He rends and tears it with his wrathful paw,
And, highly scorning that the lowly earth
Should drink his blood, mounts up into the air.
And so it fares with me, whose dauntless mind   15
The ambitious Mortimer would seek to curb,
And that unnatural Queen, false Isabel,
That thus hath pent and mewed me in a prison.
For such outrageous passions cloy my soul,
As with the wings of rancour and disdain   20

---

  0   sd ed. (*Enter the king, Leicester, with a Bishop / for the crowne.* Q).
  3   *lay* stayed, resided.
       a space an interval, period of time.
  8   *private men* i.e. those not holding public office.
       allayed diluted, abated.
9–10   *forest deer . . . wounds* Cf the belief that the stag, when wounded by an arrow, would
       eat the herb dittany; this would close the wound, forcing the arrow out (Pliny,
       Naturalis Historia VIII.xli.97).
 13   *And,* ed. (not in Q).
 14   *mounts up* rises.
 18   *pent* shut up.
       mewed caged. Commonly used as a metaphor for imprisonment, a 'mew' was a cage
       or coop in which animals and birds were kept when being fattened for slaughter.
 19   *outrageous* excessive.

103

Full often am I soaring up to heaven
To plain me to the gods against them both.
But when I call to mind I am a king,
Methinks I should revenge me of the wrongs
That Mortimer and Isabel have done.   25
But what are kings, when regiment is gone,
But perfect shadows in a sunshine day?
My nobles rule; I bear the name of King.
I wear the crown, but am controlled by them –
By Mortimer and my unconstant Queen   30
Who spots my nuptial bed with infamy.
Whilst I am lodged within this cave of care,
Where sorrow at my elbow still attends
To company my heart with sad laments,
That bleeds within me for this strange exchange.   35
But tell me, must I now resign my crown
To make usurping Mortimer a king?

BISHOP OF WINCHESTER

Your grace mistakes; it is for England's good
And princely Edward's right we crave the crown.

EDWARD

No, 'tis for Mortimer, not Edward's head,   40
For he's a lamb encompassèd by wolves
Which in a moment will abridge his life.
But if proud Mortimer do wear this crown,
Heavens turn it to a blaze of quenchless fire,
Or, like the snaky wreath of Tisiphon,   45
Engirt the temples of his hateful head;
So shall not England's vines be perishèd,
But Edward's name survives, though Edward dies.

22   *plain* complain.
26   *regiment* rule, power.
27   *perfect* mere (Rowland).
30   *unconstant* unfaithful.
34   *company* accompany.
35   *strange exchange* i.e. the change of circumstances not becoming to a king.
41   *lamb . . . by wolves* Cf. *3 Henry VI*, 'Such safety finds / The trembling lamb environed
        with wolves' (I.i.242–3).
43–4   *crown . . . quenchless fire* Cf. Euripides' *Medea* (1186 ff.) in which Jason deserts Medea
        for Creusa. Medea exacts her revenge by giving Creusa a golden crown which bursts
        into flames.
45   *Tisiphon* Tisiphone, one of the Furies (see 4.317 n.), whose hair was made of snakes.
47   *vines* The vine was the emblem of regal lineage.

LEICESTER

My lord, why waste you thus the time away?
They stay your answer: will you yield your crown?   50

EDWARD

Ah Leicester, weigh how hardly I can brook
To lose my crown and kingdom without cause,
To give ambitious Mortimer my right,
That like a mountain overwhelms my bliss;
In which extreme my mind here murdered is.   55
But what the heavens appoint, I must obey.

                        [*He removes his crown*]

Here, take my crown – the life of Edward too.
Two kings in England cannot reign at once.
But stay awhile; let me be King till night,
That I may gaze upon this glittering crown;   60
So shall my eyes receive their last content,
My head, the latest honour due to it,
And jointly both yield up their wishèd right.
Continue ever, thou celestial sun;
Let never silent night possess this clime.   65
Stand still, you watches of the element;
All times and seasons rest you at a stay,
That Edward may be still fair England's King.
But day's bright beams doth vanish fast away,
And needs I must resign my wishèd crown.   70
Inhuman creatures, nursed with tiger's milk,
Why gape you for your sovereign's overthrow?
My diadem, I mean, and guiltless life.
See, monsters, see, I'll wear my crown again.

                        [*He puts on the crown*]

What, fear you not the fury of your King?   75

---

50   *stay* await.
50–111 Shakespeare was substantially indebted to this passage in the deposition scene (IV.i)
        of *Richard II*.
51   *weigh* ed. (way Q1–2; waigh Q3–4).
64–8   Cf. Faustus' last speech (*Dr Faustus*, V.ii) in which he desperately hopes to escape the
        mutable effects of time and forestall his imminent demise.
66   *watches . . . element* the stars and planets of the sky. The 'watches' are the four parts
        of the night, while the 'element' is the sky.
67   *rest . . . a stay* i.e. remain fixed.
71   *tiger's milk* It was commonly believed that human moral characteristics were acquired
        from the mother through weaning; the tiger was a byword for cruelty.

But hapless Edward, thou art fondly led.
They pass not for thy frowns as late they did,
But seek to make a new-elected king,
Which fills my mind with strange despairing thoughts,
Which thoughts are martyred with endless torments;   80
And in this torment, comfort find I none
But that I feel the crown upon my head.
And therefore let me wear it yet a while.

TRUSSEL

My lord, the parliament must have present news,
And therefore say, will you resign or no?   85

The King rageth

EDWARD

I'll not resign, but whilst I live –
Traitors, be gone, and join you with Mortimer.
Elect, conspire, install, do what you will;
Their blood and yours shall seal these treacheries.

BISHOP OF WINCHESTER

This answer we'll return, and so farewell.   90

[*The* BISHOP OF WINCHESTER *and* TRUSSEL *begin to leave*]

LEICESTER

Call them again, my lord, and speak them fair,
For if they go, the Prince shall lose his right.

EDWARD

Call thou them back; I have no power to speak.

LEICESTER

My lord, the King is willing to resign.

BISHOP OF WINCHESTER

If he be not, let him choose –   95

EDWARD

O would I might! But heavens and earth conspire
To make me miserable.   [*He removes the crown*]
          Here, receive my crown.
Receive it? No, these innocent hands of mine

---

76   *fondly* foolishly.
77   *pass* care.
       late i.e. recently.
78   *seek* ed. (seekes Q).
86   The line is metrically short. Some editors emend to supply the missing foot ('be
       King'), but the Q reading can be interpreted as portraying Edward's exasperated
       inarticulacy.
88   *install* invest, place (someone) in authority.

Shall not be guilty of so foul a crime.
He of you all that most desires my blood   100
And will be called the murderer of a king.
Take it. What, are you moved? Pity you me?
Then send for unrelenting Mortimer
And Isabel, whose eyes, being turned to steel,
Will sooner sparkle fire than shed a tear.   105
Yet stay, for rather than I will look on them,
Here, here!   [*He gives the crown to the* BISHOP]
              Now, sweet God of heaven,
Make me despise this transitory pomp,
And sit for aye enthronizèd in heaven,
Come death, and with thy fingers close my eyes,   110
Or if I live, let me forget myself.

BISHOP OF WINCHESTER
My lord.

EDWARD
Call me not lord! Away, out of my sight!
Ah, pardon me; grief makes me lunatic.
Let not that Mortimer protect my son;   115
More safety is there in a tiger's jaws
Than his embracements.   [*He gives a handkerchief*]
              Bear this to the Queen,
Wet with my tears and dried again with sighs.
If with the sight thereof she be not moved.
Return it back and dip it in my blood.   120
Commend me to my son, and bid him rule
Better than I. Yet how have I transgressed,
Unless it be with too much clemency?

TRUSSEL
And thus, most humbly, do we take our leave.

EDWARD
Farewell. I know the next news that they bring   125
Will be my death, and welcome shall it be;

105   *sparkle fire* flash with anger or rage, like sparks struck from steel by friction.
109   *for aye* for ever.
         enthronizèd enthroned.
111   ed. (*Enter Bartley* Q; sd moved to line 127 in this edn).
112   sp BISHOP OF WINCHESTER ed. (*Bartley* Q).
113–14 ed. (Call . . . lorde, / Away . . . me, / Greefe . . . lunatick, Q).
115   *protect* be protector to.
117   *Than* ed. (This Q).

To wretched men death is felicity.

[*Enter* BERKELEY *with a letter*]

LEICESTER

Another post. What news brings he?

EDWARD

Such news as I expect. Come, Berkeley, come,

And tell thy message to my naked breast. 130

BERKELEY

My lord, think not a thought so villainous

Can harbour in a man of noble birth.

To do your highness service and devoir,

And save you from your foes, Berkeley would die.

LEICESTER [*Reading the letter*]

My lord, the council of the Queen commands 135

That I resign my charge.

EDWARD

And who must keep me now? Must you, my lord?

BERKELEY

Ay, my most gracious lord, so 'tis decreed.

EDWARD [*Taking the letter*]

By Mortimer, whose name is written here.

[*He tears up the letter*]

Well may I rend his name that rends my heart! 140

This poor revenge hath something eased my mind.

So may his limbs be torn, as is this paper!

Hear me, immortal Jove, and grant it too.

BERKELEY

Your grace must hence with me to Berkeley straight.

EDWARD

Whither you will; all places are alike, 145

And every earth is fit for burial.

LEICESTER

Favour him, my lord, as much as lieth in you.

BERKELEY

Even so betide my soul as I use him.

---

130   *naked breast* Many editors argue that Edward is 'offering himself as to a murderer's dagger' (Gill).

131   sp BERKELEY ed. (*Bartley* Q; and throughout).

133   *devoir* duty.

143   *Jove* or Jupiter, the supreme god in the Roman pantheon.

EDWARD

    Mine enemy hath pitied my estate,

    And that's the cause that I am now removed.   150

BERKELEY

    And thinks your grace that Berkeley will be cruel?

EDWARD

    I know not; but of this am I assured,

    That death ends all, and I can die but once.

    Leicester, farewell.

LEICESTER

    Not yet, my lord; I'll bear you on your way.   155

Exeunt

[SCENE 21]

Enter MORTIMER [JUNIOR], *and Queen* ISABELLA

MORTIMER JUNIOR

    Fair Isabel, now have we our desire.

    The proud corrupters of the light-brained King

    Have done their homage to the lofty gallows,

    And he himself lies in captivity.

    Be ruled by me, and we will rule the realm.   5

    In any case, take heed of childish fear,

    For now we hold an old wolf by the ears,

    That if he slip will seize upon us both,

    And gripe the sorer, being griped himself.

    Think therefore, madam, that imports us much   10

    To erect your son with all the speed we may,

---

149   *estate* condition.
153   *I . . . once* proverbial (Tilley M 219).

  2   *light-brained* frivolous, wanton.
  7   *hold . . . ears* proverbial (Tilley W 603).
  9   *gripe . . . sorer* i.e. will seize upon (us) more grievously.
       griped afflicted.
 10 *imports us much* i.e. it is most important for us (*us* ed.; as Q).
 11 *erect* establish on the throne.

And that I be Protector over him,
For our behoof will bear the greater sway
Whenas a king's name shall be underwrit.

ISABELLA
Sweet Mortimer, the life of Isabel,   15
Be thou persuaded that I love thee well,
And therefore, so the Prince my son be safe,
Whom I esteem as dear as these mine eyes,
Conclude against his father what thou wilt,
And I myself will willingly subscribe.   20

MORTIMER JUNIOR
First would I hear news that he were deposed,
And then let me alone to handle him.

Enter MESSENGER

MORTIMER JUNIOR
Letters, from whence?

MESSENGER   From Kenilworth, my lord.

ISABELLA
How fares my lord the King?

MESSENGER
In health, madam, but full of pensiveness.   25

ISABELLA
Alas, poor soul, would I could ease his grief.

[*Enter the* BISHOP OF WINCHESTER *with the crown*]

Thanks, gentle Winchester.
[*To the* MESSENGER]   Sirrah, be gone.

[*Exit* MESSENGER]

BISHOP OF WINCHESTER
The King hath willingly resigned his crown.

ISABELLA
O happy news! Send for the Prince, my son.

BISHOP OF WINCHESTER
Further, ere this letter was sealed, Lord Berkeley came,   30

13–14   i.e. Mortimer and the queen will have greater authority when he can act in the king's
        name (literally, sign official documents as if he were the king).
18   *as dear . . . eyes* proverbial (Dent E 249).
19   *Conclude* i.e. make a final decision about the king's fate.
22   *let me alone* trust me.
25   *pensiveness* sadness, melancholy.
30   sp BISHOP OF WINCHESTER ed. (*Bish* Q; and throughout the scene).
        ere ed. (or Q).

So that he now is gone from Kenilworth.
And we have heard that Edmund laid a plot
To set his brother free; no more but so.
The lord of Berkeley is so pitiful
As Leicester that had charge of him before. 35
ISABELLA
Then let some other be his guardian.
[*Exit* BISHOP OF WINCHESTER]
MORTIMER JUNIOR
Let me alone – here is the privy seal.
[*Calls offstage*]
Who's there? Call hither Gourney and Maltravers.
To dash the heavy-headed Edmund's drift,
Berkeley shall be discharged, the King removed, 40
And none but we shall know where he lieth.
ISABELLA
But Mortimer, as long as he survives
What safety rests for us, or for my son?
MORTIMER JUNIOR
Speak, shall he presently be dispatched and die?
ISABELLA
I would he were, so it were not by my means. 45

Enter MALTRAVERS *and* GOURNEY

MORTIMER JUNIOR
Enough. Maltravers, write a letter presently
Unto the Lord of Berkeley from ourself,
That he resign the King to thee and Gourney;
And when 'tis done, we will subscribe our name.
MALTRAVERS
It shall be done, my lord.
MORTIMER JUNIOR   Gourney.
GOURNEY   My lord? 50
MORTIMER JUNIOR

39   *dash* frustrate.
      heavy-headed stupid, dull.
      drift plot, scheme.
43   *rests* remains.
44   *dispatched* killed.
48   *resign* surrender.

As thou intendest to rise by Mortimer,
Who now makes Fortune's wheel turn as he please,
Seek all the means thou canst to make him droop,
And neither give him kind word nor good look.

GOURNEY

I warrant you, my lord.   55

MORTIMER JUNIOR

And this above the rest, because we hear
That Edmund casts to work his liberty,
Remove him still from place to place by night,
And at the last he come to Kenilworth,
And then from thence to Berkeley back again.   60
And by the way to make him fret the more,
Speak curstly to him; and in any case
Let no man comfort him if he chance to weep,
But amplify his grief with bitter words.

MALTRAVERS

Fear not, my lord, we'll do as you command.   65

MORTIMER JUNIOR

So now away; post thitherwards amain.

ISABELLA

Whither goes this letter? To my lord the King?
Commend me humbly to his majesty,
And tell him that I labour all in vain
To ease his grief and work his liberty.   ·   70
And bear him this, as witness of my love.

> *[She gives* MALTRAVERS *a jewel]*

MALTRAVERS

I will, madam.

> *Exeunt* MALTRAVERS *and* GOURNEY.
> ISABELLA *and* MORTIMER *[*JUNIOR*] remain*

> *Enter the young* PRINCE [EDWARD],
> *and the* EARL OF KENT *talking with him*

---

52   *Fortune's wheel . . . please* In sixteenth-century iconography, Fortune was represented
      by a wheel whose turning determined human fate; here Mortimer Junior arrogates
      that power to himself. Cf. *1 Tamburlaine,* 'I hold the Fates bound fast in iron chains
      / And with my hand turn Fortune's wheel about' (I.ii.174–5).
57   *casts* plans.
62   *curstly* malevolently, uncivilly.
66   *post thitherwards amain* go there speedily.

MORTIMER JUNIOR [*Aside to* ISABELLA]
　　Finely dissembled; do so still, sweet Queen.
　　Here comes the young Prince with the Earl of Kent.
ISABELLA [*Aside to* MORTIMER JUNIOR]
　　Something he whispers in his childish ears.　　　　　　75
MORTIMER JUNIOR [*Aside*]
　　If he have such access unto the Prince,
　　Our plots and stratagems will soon be dashed.
ISABELLA [*Aside*]
　　Use Edmund friendly, as if all were well.
MORTIMER JUNIOR
　　How fares my honourable lord of Kent?
KENT
　　In health, sweet Mortimer. How fares your grace?　　80
ISABELLA
　　Well – if my lord your brother were enlarged.
KENT
　　I hear of late he hath deposed himself.
ISABELLA
　　The more my grief.
MORTIMER JUNIOR
　　And mine.
KENT [*Aside*]
　　Ah, they do dissemble.　　　　　　　　　　　　　　　85
ISABELLA
　　Sweet son, come hither; I must talk with thee.
MORTIMER JUNIOR
　　Thou, being his uncle and the next of blood,
　　Do look to be Protector over the Prince.
KENT
　　Not I, my lord; who should protect the son
　　But she that gave him life – I mean, the Queen?　　90
PRINCE EDWARD
　　Mother, persuade me not to wear the crown;
　　Let him be King. I am too young to reign.
ISABELLA
　　But be content, seeing it his highness' pleasure.

73　　*dissembled* feigned.
81　　*enlarged* released.
92　　*him* i.e. the Prince's father, Edward II.

113

PRINCE EDWARD

  Let me but see him first, and then I will.

KENT

  Ay, do, sweet nephew.   95

ISABELLA

  Brother, you know it is impossible.

PRINCE EDWARD

  Why, is he dead?

ISABELLA

  No, God forbid.

KENT

  I would those words proceeded from your heart.

MORTIMER JUNIOR

  Inconstant Edmund, dost thou favour him   100

  That wast a cause of his imprisonment?

KENT

  The more cause have I now to make amends.

MORTIMER JUNIOR

  I tell thee 'tis not meet that one so false

  Should come about the person of a prince.

  My lord, he hath betrayed the King, his brother,   105

  And therefore trust him not.

PRINCE EDWARD

  But he repents and sorrows for it now.

ISABELLA

  Come son, and go with this gentle lord and me.

PRINCE EDWARD

  With you I will, but not with Mortimer.

MORTIMER JUNIOR

  Why, youngling, 'sdain'st thou so of Mortimer?   110

  Then I will carry thee by force away.

PRINCE EDWARD

  Help, uncle Kent, Mortimer will wrong me.

              [*Exit* MORTIMER JUNIOR *with* PRINCE EDWARD]

ISABELLA

  Brother Edmund, strive not; we are his friends.

  Isabel is nearer than the Earl of Kent.

---

103   *meet* proper, appropriate.

110   *youngling* stripling, novice (often spoken in a condescending manner).

       'sdain'st contracted form of 'disdainest'.

KENT

    Sister, Edward is my charge; redeem him.   115

ISABELLA

    Edward is my son, and I will keep him.   [*Exit*]

KENT

    Mortimer shall know that he hath wronged me.

    Hence will I haste to Kenilworth Castle

    And rescue agèd Edward from his foes,

    To be revenged on Mortimer and thee.   [*Exit*] 120

[SCENE 22]

Enter MALTRAVERS *and* GOURNEY [*carrying torches,*]
with [EDWARD] *the King*[*, and soldiers*]

MALTRAVERS

    My lord, be not pensive; we are your friends.

    Men are ordained to live in misery;

    Therefore come, dalliance dangereth our lives.

EDWARD

    Friends, whither must unhappy Edward go?

    Will hateful Mortimer appoint no rest?   5

    Must I be vexèd like the nightly bird

    Whose sight is loathsome to all winged fowls?

    When will the fury of his mind assuage?

    When will his heart be satisfied with blood?

    If mine will serve, unbowel straight this breast,   10

115   *charge* responsibility.
        redeem him i.e. return him.
119   *agèd Edward* Presumably the adjective serves to differentiate him from his son,
        Prince Edward; the historical Edward II was, at this point, only 43 years old.
120   sd ed. (*Exeunt omnes.* Q).

1   *pensive* full of sorrow.
3   *dalliance* idle delay.
4   *unhappy* unfortunate.
6   *vexèd* tormented.
    nightly bird i.e. the owl (a common portent of death).
10   *unbowel* open up.
    straight without delay.

And give my heart to Isabel and him;
It is the chiefest mark they level at.

GOURNEY

Not so, my liege; the Queen hath given this charge
To keep your grace in safety.
Your passions make your dolours to increase.   15

EDWARD

This usage makes my misery increase.
But can my air of life continue long
When all my senses are annoyed with stench?
Within a dungeon England's King is kept,
Where I am starved for want of sustenance.   20
My daily diet is heart-breaking sobs,
That almost rends the closet of my heart.
Thus lives old Edward, not relieved by any.
And so must die, though pitièd by many.
O water, gentle friends, to cool my thirst   25
And clear my body from foul excrements.

MALTRAVERS

Here's channel water, as our charge is given;
Sit down, for we'll be barbers to your grace.

EDWARD

Traitors, away! What, will you murder me,
Or choke your sovereign with puddle water?   30

GOURNEY

No, but wash your face and shave away your beard,
Lest you be known and so be rescuèd.

MALTRAVERS

Why strive you thus? Your labour is in vain.

EDWARD

The wren may strive against the lion's strength,
But all in vain; so vainly do I strive   35
To seek for mercy at a tyrant's hand.

> *They wash him with puddle water,*
> *and shave his beard away*

---

12   *mark* target.
      level aim.
17   *air of life* breath.
22   *closet* private chamber.
26   *excrements* faeces. (The word also carried the archaic sense of 'hair', which Maltravers
      and Gourney take – by deliberate error – to be Edward's meaning.)
27   *channel* drain, sewer. Cf. 1.187.

Immortal powers, that knows the painful cares
That waits upon my poor distressèd soul,
O level all your looks upon these daring men,
That wrongs their liege and sovereign, England's King.   40
O Gaveston, it is for thee that I am wronged;
For me, both thou and both the Spencers died,
And for your sakes a thousand wrongs I'll take.
The Spencers' ghosts, wherever they remain,
Wish well to mine; then tush, for them I'll die.   45

MALTRAVERS

'Twixt theirs and yours shall be no enmity.
Come, come away. Now put the torches out;
We'll enter in by darkness to Kenilworth.

Enter EDMUND [*the* EARL OF KENT]

GOURNEY

How now, who comes there?

MALTRAVERS

Guard the King sure; it is the Earl of Kent.   50

EDWARD

O gentle brother, help to rescue me.

MALTRAVERS

Keep them asunder; thrust in the King.

KENT

Soldiers, let me but talk to him one word.

GOURNEY

Lay hands upon the Earl for this assault.

KENT

Lay down your weapons; traitors, yield the King!   55

MALTRAVERS

Edmund, yield thou thyself, or thou shalt die.

[*Soldiers seize* KENT]

KENT

Base villains, wherefore do you grip me thus?

GOURNEY

Bind him, and so convey him to the court.

37–9   Forker compares Thomas Lodge's *Wounds of Civil War* (1588), 'Immortal powers
that know the painful cares / That weight upon my poor distressed heart, / O bend
your brows and level all your looks / Of dreadful awe upon these daring men'
(IV.ii.87–90).

44   *remain* dwell.

117

EDMUND

    Where is the court but here? Here is the King,

    And I will visit him. Why stay you me?   60

MALTRAVERS

    The court is where Lord Mortimer remains.

    Thither shall your honour go; and so, farewell.

            Exeunt MALTRAVERS *and* GOURNEY, *with* [EDWARD]

            the King. EDMUND [*the* EARL OF KENT] *and*

            the soldiers [*remain*]

KENT

    O, miserable is that commonweal, where lords

    Keep courts and kings are locked in prison!

SOLDIER

    Wherefore stay we? On, sirs, to the court.   65

KENT

    Ay, lead me whither you will, even to my death,

    Seeing that my brother cannot be released.

                      Exeunt

[SCENE 23]

Enter MORTIMER [JUNIOR] *alone*

MORTIMER JUNIOR

    The King must die, or Mortimer goes down;

    The commons now begin to pity him.

    Yet he that is the cause of Edward's death

    Is sure to pay for it when his son is of age,

    And therefore will I do it cunningly.   5

    This letter, written by a friend of ours,

    Contains his death, yet bids them save his life:

    [*He reads*] 'Edwardum occidere nolite timere, bonum est,

    Fear not to kill the King, 'tis good he die.'

    But read it thus, and that's another sense: 10

---

59   *Where . . . but here* In the sixteenth century the court was understood not only as a
       fixed location but as the establishment which accompanied the person of the king.

63   *commonweal* state.

'*Edwardum occidere nolite, timere bonum est,*
Kill not the King, 'tis good to fear the worst.'
Unpointed as it is, thus shall it go,
That, being dead, if it chance to be found,
Maltravers and the rest may bear the blame,   15
And we be quit that caused it to be done.
Within this room is locked the messenger
That shall convey it and perform the rest.
And by a secret token that he bears,
Shall he be murdered when the deed is done.   20
Lightborne, come forth.

                    [*Enter* LIGHTBORNE]

Art thou as resolute as thou wast?
LIGHTBORNE
What else, my lord? And far more resolute.
MORTIMER JUNIOR
And hast thou cast how to accomplish it?
LIGHTBORNE
Ay, ay, and none shall know which way he died.
MORTIMER JUNIOR
But at his looks, Lightborne, thou wilt relent.   25
LIGHTBORNE
Relent? Ha, ha! I use much to relent.
MORTIMER JUNIOR
Well, do it bravely, and be secret.
LIGHTBORNE
You shall not need to give instructions;
'Tis not the first time I have killed a man.

---

13   *Unpointed* unpunctuated. The letter's meaning is made ambiguous through its lack
     of punctuation; this is intended to obscure Mortimer Junior's involvement in
     Edward's death.
14   *being dead* i.e. once Edward is murdered.
16   *quit* acquitted, exonerated.
21   *Lightborne* The assassin derives from theatrical and not historical sources; such
     characters were popular in tragedies of the late 1580s and early 1590s. It is significant
     that he shares his name (which Anglicizes Lucifer) with one of Satan's associates in
     the Chester cycle of mystery plays (*c.* 1467–88): according to a well-known saying
     of the time, 'An Englishman Italianate is the Devil incarnate.'
26   *use much* i.e. am accustomed to (spoken facetiously).
27   *bravely* (i) without fear (ii) excellently, finely.

I learned in Naples how to poison flowers, 30
To strangle with a lawn thrust through the throat,
To pierce the windpipe with a needle's point,
Or, whilst one is asleep, to take a quill
And blow a little powder in his ears,
Or open his mouth and pour quicksilver down. 35
But yet I have a braver way than these.

MORTIMER JUNIOR
What's that?

LIGHTBORNE
Nay, you shall pardon me; none shall know my tricks.

MORTIMER JUNIOR
I care not how it is, so it be not spied.
Deliver this to Gourney and Maltravers. 40
[*He gives the letter to* LIGHTBORNE]
At every ten miles' end thou hast a horse.
[*Giving a token*] Take this. Away, and never see me more.

LIGHTBORNE
No?

MORTIMER JUNIOR
No, unless thou bring me news of Edward's death.

LIGHTBORNE
That will I quickly do. Farewell, my lord. [*Exit*] 45

MORTIMER JUNIOR
The Prince I rule, the Queen do I command,
And with a lowly congé to the ground
The proudest lords salute me as I pass;
I seal, I cancel, I do what I will.

30–6   *I learned . . . these* Lightborne's account of his studies in Naples – reputedly the most
dangerous of Italian cities – may recall a panic of late 1591 about a trained Italian
assassin being sent to England to assassinate the queen. Cf. also *The Jew of Malta*, 'I
learned in Florence how to kiss my hand' (II.iii.23), 'I walk abroad a-nights / And kill
sick people groaning under walls; / Sometimes I go about and poison wells . . .'
(II.iii.175–7).

31   *lawn . . . throat* a piece of fine linen cloth forced down the victim's throat to block
the windpipe.

34   *powder in his ears* Cf. the murder of Hamlet's father in Shakespeare's play (I.v.61–70).

35   *quicksilver* mercury (which is poisonous).

36   *braver* more skilful.

38   *tricks* skills, methods.

42   *Take this* i.e. the 'secret token' (19) which will seal Lightborne's fate.

47   *congé* bow.

49   *seal* authorize official documents.

Feared am I more than loved; let me be feared,　　　　　50
And when I frown, make all the court look pale.
I view the Prince with Aristarchus' eyes,
Whose looks were as a breeching to a boy.
They thrust upon me the protectorship
And sue to me for that that I desire.　　　　　55
While at the council table, grave enough,
And not unlike a bashful Puritan,
First I complain of imbecility,
Saying it is *onus quam gravissimum*,
Till being interrupted by my friends,　　　　　60
Suscepi that *provinciam*, as they term it,
And to conclude, I am Protector now.
Now is all sure: the Queen and Mortimer
Shall rule the realm, the King, and none rule us.
Mine enemies will I plague, my friends advance,　　　　　65
And what I list command, who dare control?
Maior sum quam cui possit fortuna nocere.
And that this be the coronation day,
It pleaseth me, and Isabel the Queen.
　　　　　　　　　　　　　[*Trumpets sound within*]
The trumpets sound; I must go take my place.　　　　　70

　　　　Enter the young King [EDWARD III],
　　BISHOP [OF CANTERBURY], CHAMPION,
　　　NOBLES, [*and*] *Queen* [ISABELLA]

50　*Feared . . . feared* Mortimer Junior follows the advice of Machiavelli's *The Prince*, a
　　forbidden book of the period which circulated surreptitiously in manuscript:
　　'because hardly can [love and fear] subsist both together, it is much safer to be feared,
　　than to be lov'd' (trans. Edward Dacres, London, 1640, XVII, p. 130).
52　*Aristarchus* notoriously harsh schoolmaster and grammarian who lived in Alex-
　　andria in the second century BC.
53　*breeching* whipping.
55　*sue to* petition.
57　*Puritan* follower of an extreme Protestant movement which emerged in the sixteenth
　　century and was theologically rooted in Calvinism. Puritans were known for their
　　hypocritical advocacy of self-restraint.
58　*imbecility* weakness.
59　*onus quam gravissimum* (Latin) a very heavy burden.
61　*Suscepi . . . provinciam* (Latin) I have undertaken that office.
66　*list* desire to.
67　*Maior sum quam cui possit fortuna nocere* I am so great that Fortune cannot harm
　　me; from Ovid's *Metamorphoses*, VI. 195.
71　sp BISHOP OF CANTERBURY ed. (*Bish.* Q).

BISHOP OF CANTERBURY

Long live King Edward, by the grace of God,
King of England and Lord of Ireland.

CHAMPION

If any Christian, Heathen, Turk, or Jew
Dares but affirm that Edward's not true King,
And will avouch his saying with the sword,   75
I am the Champion that will combat him.   [*Silence*]

MORTIMER JUNIOR

None comes. Sound trumpets.   [*Trumpets sound*]

KING EDWARD III   Champion, here's to thee.
                                        [*He raises his goblet*]

ISABELLA

Lord Mortimer, now take him to your charge.

Enter SOLDIERS *with the* EARL OF KENT *prisoner*

MORTIMER JUNIOR

What traitor have we there with blades and bills?

SOLDIER

Edmund, the Earl of Kent.

KING EDWARD III   What hath he done?   80

SOLDIER

A would have taken the King away perforce,
As we were bringing him to Kenilworth.

MORTIMER JUNIOR

Did you attempt his rescue, Edmund? Speak.

KENT

Mortimer, I did; he is our King,
And thou compell'st this prince to wear the crown.   85

MORTIMER JUNIOR

Strike off his head! He shall have martial law.

KENT

Strike off my head? Base traitor, I defy thee.

KING EDWARD III

My lord, he is my uncle and shall live.

MORTIMER JUNIOR

My lord, he is your enemy and shall die.

---

77   sp KING EDWARD III ed. (*King.* Q; and throughout).
79   *blades and bills* swords and halberds.
81   *perforce* by force, violently.
86   *martial law* (here) summary execution without trial.

KENT

Stay, villains. 90

KING EDWARD III

Sweet mother, if I cannot pardon him,

Entreat my Lord Protector for his life.

ISABELLA

Son, be content; I dare not speak a word.

KING EDWARD III

Nor I, and yet methinks I should command;

But seeing I cannot, I'll entreat for him. 95

My lord, if you will let my uncle live,

I will requite it when I come to age.

MORTIMER JUNIOR

'Tis for your highness' good, and for the realm's.

[*To* SOLDIERS] How often shall I bid you bear him hence?

KENT

Art thou King? Must I die at thy command? 100

MORTIMER JUNIOR

At our command. Once more, away with him.

KENT

Let me but stay and speak; I will not go.

Either my brother or his son is King,

And none of both them thirst for Edmund's blood.

And therefore, soldiers, whither will you hale me? 105

> *They hale* EDMUND [*the* EARL OF KENT] *away,*
> *and carry him to be beheaded*

> [*Exit* MORTIMER JUNIOR *with attendants,*
> BISHOP OF CANTERBURY, NOBLES, CHAMPION.
> KING EDWARD III *and* ISABELLA *remain*]

KING EDWARD III

What safety may I look for at his hands,

If that my uncle shall be murdered thus?

ISABELLA

Fear not, sweet boy, I'll guard thee from thy foes.

Had Edmund lived, he would have sought thy death.

Come son, we'll ride a-hunting in the park. 110

---

101 *our command* The text is ambiguous: the emphasis on 'our' can suggest Mortimer's
responsible action as Protector, jointly with the queen; but it can also suggest his
overweening ambition in adopting the royal plural.

104 *none of both them* ed. (none of both, then Q) i.e. neither of them.

KING EDWARD III
    And shall my uncle Edmund ride with us?
ISABELLA
    He is a traitor; think not on him. Come.

Exeunt

[SCENE 24]

Enter MALTRAVERS *and* GOURNEY

MALTRAVERS
    Gourney, I wonder the King dies not.
    Being in a vault up to the knees in water,
    To which the channels of the castle run,
    From whence a damp continually ariseth
    That were enough to poison any man,   5
    Much more a king, brought up so tenderly.
GOURNEY
    And so do I, Maltravers. Yesternight
    I opened but the door to throw him meat.
    And I was almost stifled with the savour.
MALTRAVERS
    He hath a body able to endure   10
    More than we can inflict; and therefore now
    Let us assail his mind another while.
GOURNEY
    Send for him out thence, and I will anger him.

Enter LIGHTBORNE

MALTRAVERS
    But stay, who's this?
LIGHTBORNE   My Lord Protector greets you.
                [*He presents them with the letter*]
GOURNEY
    What's here? I know not how to construe it.   15

   4   *damp* fog, mist.
   8   meat food.
   9   *savour* smell, stench.
  13   sd ed.; after line 14 in Q.

MALTRAVERS

    Gourney, it was left unpointed for the nonce:

    [*Reading*] '*Edwardum occidere nolite timere*' –

    That's his meaning.

LIGHTBORNE [*Showing the token*]

    Know you this token? I must have the King.

MALTRAVERS

    Ay, stay a while; thou shalt have answer straight.   20

    [*Aside to* GOURNEY] This villain's sent to make away the King.

GOURNEY [*Aside to* MALTRAVERS]

    I thought as much.

MALTRAVERS [*Aside to* GOURNEY] And when the murder's done,

    See how he must be handled for his labour.

    Pereat iste! Let him have the King.

    What else? [*To* LIGHTBORNE] Here is the keys; this is the lake.   25

    Do as you are commanded by my lord.

LIGHTBORNE

    I know what I must do; get you away –

    Yet be not far off; I shall need your help.

    See that in the next room I have a fire,

    And get me a spit, and let it be red hot.   30

MALTRAVERS

    Very well.

GOURNEY

    Need you anything besides?

LIGHTBORNE

    What else? A table and a featherbed.

GOURNEY

    That's all?

LIGHTBORNE

    Ay, ay; so when I call you, bring it in.   35

MALTRAVERS

    Fear not you that.

---

16   *unpointed* unpunctuated.

       for the nonce for the purpose in hand.

21   *make away* i.e. murder.

24   *Pereat iste!* Let him die!

25   *lake* dungeon; also associated with hell. Cf. *2 Tamburlaine*, 'And travel headlong to the lake of hell' (III.v.24).

33   *featherbed* stuffed palliasse; see notes on ll. 71 and 112.

GOURNEY

Here's a light to go into the dungeon.

                         [*Exit* MALTRAVERS *and* GOURNEY]

LIGHTBORNE

So now must I about this gear; ne'er was there any
So finely handled as this king shall be.
Foh! Here's a place indeed with all my heart.   40

                  [*Enter* EDWARD]

EDWARD

Who's there? What light is that? Wherefore comes thou?

LIGHTBORNE

To comfort you and bring you joyful news.

EDWARD

Small comfort finds poor Edward in thy looks.
Villain, I know thou com'st to murder me.

LIGHTBORNE

To murder you, my most gracious lord?   45
Far is it from my heart to do you harm.
The Queen sent me to see how you were used,
For she relents at this your misery.
And what eyes can refrain from shedding tears
To see a king in this most piteous state?   50

EDWARD

Weep'st thou already? List awhile to me,
And then thy heart, were it as Gourney's is,
Or as Maltravers', hewn from the Caucasus,
Yet will it melt ere I have done my tale.

---

38   *about* i.e. proceed with, get on with.
      gear business.

40   *Foh!* Lightborne is affected by the stench of the dungeon.
      with all my heart i.e. I must say (Bevington and Rasmussen).

40   sd Q gives no stage direction for Edward to enter, which may indicate that the entry
      was unconventional and possibly not under the prompter's direct control. An attrac-
      tive possibility is that the dungeon is imagined to be located in the under-stage area
      (often referred to as 'hell'), and that Lightborne reveals Edward by opening a trap-
      door at line 40; he would then emerge through it at some point in the ensuing
      dialogue. (Line 58 suggests that he is no longer in his dungeon.) Alternatively, some
      editors have assumed that he is 'discovered', i.e. revealed when a traverse curtain is
      drawn back at the rear of the stage.

47   *used* i.e. being treated.

51   *List* listen.

53   *Caucasus* the mountain range between the Black and Caspian Seas known for its
      harsh terrain and bitterly cold climate.

This dungeon where they keep me is the sink   55
Wherein the filth of all the castle falls.

LIGHTBORNE

O villains!

EDWARD

And there in mire and puddle have I stood
This ten days' space; and lest that I should sleep,
One plays continually upon a drum.   60
They give me bread and water, being a king,
So that for want of sleep and sustenance
My mind's distempered and my body's numbed,
And whether I have limbs or no, I know not.
O, would my blood dropped out from every vein,   65
As doth this water from my tattered robes.
Tell Isabel the Queen I looked not thus
When for her sake I ran at tilt in France
And there unhorsed the Duke of Cleremont.

LIGHTBORNE

O speak no more, my lord; this breaks my heart.   70
Lie on this bed and rest yourself awhile.

EDWARD

These looks of thine can harbour nought but death.
I see my tragedy written in thy brows.
Yet stay awhile; forbear thy bloody hand,
And let me see the stroke before it comes,   75
That even then when I shall lose my life,
My mind may be more steadfast on my God.

LIGHTBORNE

What means your highness to mistrust me thus?

EDWARD

What means thou to dissemble with me thus?

---

55   *sink* cess-pool.
56   *filth* sewage.
63   *distempered* deranged, mentally disturbed.
64   *no* not.
68–9 an invented incident not recounted in the chronicles.
68   *ran at tilt* jousted.
71   *this bed* i.e. the 'featherbed' called for by Lightborne at line 33. The text gives no
      indication of how and when the prop should be brought on stage.
73   *tragedy* destruction.
76   *That even* ed. (That and euen Q).

LIGHTBORNE

> These hands were never stained with innocent blood,   80
> Nor shall they now be tainted with a king's.

EDWARD

> Forgive my thought, for having such a thought.
> One jewel have I left; receive thou this.
> Still fear I, and I know not what's the cause,
> But every joint shakes as I give it thee.   85
> O if thou harbour'st murder in thy heart,
> Let this gift change thy mind and save thy soul.
> Know that I am a king – O, at that name,
> I feel a hell of grief. Where is my crown?
> Gone, gone. And do I remain alive?   90

LIGHTBORNE

> You're overwatched, my lord; lie down and rest.

EDWARD

> But that grief keeps me waking, I should sleep;
> For not these ten days have these eyes' lids closed.
> Now as I speak they fall, and yet with fear
> Open again. O wherefore sits thou here?   95

LIGHTBORNE

> If you mistrust me, I'll be gone, my lord.

EDWARD

> No, no, for if thou mean'st to murder me,
> Thou wilt return again, and therefore stay.   [*He falls asleep*]

LIGHTBORNE

> He sleeps.

EDWARD [*Starting*]

> O let me not die! Yet stay, O stay awhile.   100

LIGHTBORNE

> How now, my lord?

EDWARD

> Something still buzzeth in mine ears
> And tells me, if I sleep I never wake.
> This fear is that which makes me tremble thus;
> And therefore tell me, wherefore art thou come?   105

---

83   *One jewel* possibly the jewel sent by the queen at 21.71; if so, Edward's handing it
       over to another potential favourite would be his final act of betrayal.
89–90 *Where . . . remain alive* A king without a crown is usually dead.
91   *overwatched* depleted through lack of sleep.
92   *grief* anxiety.
102   *buzzeth* whispers.

LIGHTBORNE

   To rid thee of thy life. Maltravers, come!

                 [*Enter* MALTRAVERS]

EDWARD

   I am too weak and feeble to resist;

   Assist me, sweet God, and receive my soul.

LIGHTBORNE

   Run for the table.

                    [*Exit* MALTRAVERS]

        [*Enter* MALTRAVERS *with* GOURNEY,
           carrying a table and hot spit]

EDWARD

   O spare me, or dispatch me in a trice!   110

LIGHTBORNE

   So, lay the table down and stamp on it;

   But not too hard, lest that you bruise his body.

          [*They seize* EDWARD *and hold him down, laying
            the table on him.* LIGHTBORNE *murders him
               with the spit. He screams and dies*]

MALTRAVERS

   I fear me that this cry will raise the town,

   And therefore let us take horse and away.

LIGHTBORNE

   Tell me, sirs, was it not bravely done?   115

GOURNEY

   Excellent well. Take this for thy reward.

             Then GOURNEY *stabs* LIGHTBORNE

---

109   sd 2 The 'featherbed' asked for at line 33 is already on stage, mentioned at line 71.
        Some editors treat that 'bed' as a separate prop, and have the featherbed for the
        murder brought on here. However, the effect of giving the two actors another bulky
        object to carry is unreasonably to slow down the action at a climactic point, with no
        covering dialogue provided by the text.

112   sd The text gives no indication as to how Lightborne uses the featherbed he asked for.
        It probably serves as a buffer to prevent bruising by direct contact with the table; if
        Edward is lying on it immediately beforehand, the murderers must first pitch him on
        to the ground. Alternatively, Lightborne may want it not for the murder itself but to
        offer Edward comfort and a false sense of security, during the preceding conversation.

115   *bravely* skilfully.

Come, let us cast the body in the moat,
And bear the King's to Mortimer, our lord.
Away!

Exeunt[, carrying the bodies]

[SCENE 25]

Enter MORTIMER [JUNIOR] *and* MALTRAVERS

MORTIMER JUNIOR
Is't done, Maltravers, and the murderer dead?
MALTRAVERS
Ay, my good lord; I would it were undone.
MORTIMER JUNIOR
Maltravers, if thou now growest penitent
I'll be thy ghostly father; therefore choose
Whether thou wilt be secret in this, 5
Or else die by the hand of Mortimer.
MALTRAVERS
Gourney, my lord, is fled, and will, I fear,
Betray us both; therefore let me fly.
MORTIMER JUNIOR
Fly to the savages!
MALTRAVERS
I humbly thank your honour. [*Exit*] 10
MORTIMER JUNIOR
As for myself, I stand as Jove's huge tree,
And others are but shrubs compared to me.
All tremble at my name, and I fear none;
Let's see who dare impeach me for his death.

Enter [ISABELLA] *the Queen*

118–19   ed. (*one line in* Q).
  119   sd ed. (*Exeunt omnes.* Q).

    4   *ghostly father* priest (who hears the confessions of those about to die).
    9   *to the savages* i.e. beyond civilization, to the wilderness.
   11   *Jove's huge tree* the oak, a byword for size and steadfastness.

ISABELLA

    Ah, Mortimer, the King my son hath news   15

    His father's dead, and we have murdered him.

MORTIMER JUNIOR

    What if he have? The King is yet a child.

ISABELLA

    Ay, ay, but he tears his hair and wrings his hands,

    And vows to be revenged upon us both.

    Into the council chamber he is gone   20

    To crave the aid and succour of his peers.

          Enter the King [EDWARD III], *with the* LORDS

                    [*and attendants*]

    Ay me, see where he comes, and they with him.

    Now, Mortimer, begins our tragedy.

FIRST LORD

    Fear not, my lord; know that you are a king.

KING EDWARD III

    Villain!   25

MORTIMER JUNIOR

    How now, my lord?

KING EDWARD III

    Think not that I am frighted with thy words.

    My father's murdered through thy treachery.

    And thou shalt die; and on his mournful hearse

    Thy hateful and accursèd head shall lie   30

    To witness to the world that by thy means

    His kingly body was too soon interred.

ISABELLA

    Weep not, sweet son.

KING EDWARD III

    Forbid not me to weep; he was my father.

    And had you loved him half so well as I,   35

    You could not bear his death thus patiently.

    But you, I fear, conspired with Mortimer.

FIRST LORD

    Why speak you not unto my lord the King?

---

17   *yet* still.

21   *succour* support.

21   sd ed.; after line 23 in Q.

24   sp FIRST LORD ed. (*Lords.* Q; also at ll. 38 and 93).

36   *patiently* calmly.

MORTIMER JUNIOR

    Because I think scorn to be accused.

    Who is the man dare say I murdered him?   40

KING EDWARD III

    Traitor, in me my loving father speaks

    And plainly saith, 'twas thou that murd'redst him.

MORTIMER JUNIOR

    But hath your grace no other proof than this?

KING EDWARD III

    Yes, if this be the hand of Mortimer.

                             [He presents the letter]

MORTIMER JUNIOR *[Aside to* ISABELLA*]*

    False Gourney hath betrayed me and himself.   45

ISABELLA *[Aside to* MORTIMER JUNIOR*]*

    I feared as much; murder cannot be hid.

MORTIMER JUNIOR

    'Tis my hand; what gather you by this?

KING EDWARD III

    That thither thou didst send a murderer.

MORTIMER JUNIOR

    What murderer? Bring forth the man I sent.

KING EDWARD III

    Ah, Mortimer, thou knowest that he is slain;   50

    And so shalt thou be too. Why stays he here?

    Bring him unto a hurdle, drag him forth;

    Hang him, I say, and set his quarters up!

    But bring his head back presently to me.

ISABELLA

    For my sake, sweet son, pity Mortimer.   55

MORTIMER JUNIOR

    Madam, entreat not; I will rather die

    Than sue for life unto a paltry boy.

KING EDWARD III

    Hence with the traitor, with the murderer.

---

41   *in me . . . speaks* 'Marlowe carefully withholds this final show of authority in the young prince until, at this point, at the death of his father, he is king in legal fact' (Merchant).

46   *murder cannot be hid* proverbial (Tilley M 1315).

52   *hurdle* frame or sledge which restrained traitors whilst being dragged through the streets to the place of execution.

53   Mortimer Junior is to be hanged, drawn, and quartered rather than merely beheaded, the privilege of aristocratic traitors granted even to Gaveston, Baldock, and the Spencers.

MORTIMER JUNIOR

    Base Fortune, now I see that in thy wheel
    There is a point to which, when men aspire,   60
    They tumble headlong down; that point I touched,
    And seeing there was no place to mount up higher,
    Why should I grieve at my declining fall?
    Farewell, fair Queen. Weep not for Mortimer,
    That scorns the world, and as a traveller   65
    Goes to discover countries yet unknown.

KING EDWARD III

    What! Suffer you the traitor to delay?
      [*Exit* MORTIMER JUNIOR, *with the* FIRST LORD *and* GUARD]

ISABELLA

    As thou received'st thy life from me,
    Spill not the blood of gentle Mortimer.

KING EDWARD III

    This argues that you spilt my father's blood,   70
    Else would you not entreat for Mortimer.

ISABELLA

    I spill his blood? No!

KING EDWARD III

    Ay, madam, you; for so the rumour runs.

ISABELLA

    That rumour is untrue; for loving thee
    Is this report raised on poor Isabel.   75

KING EDWARD III

    I do not think her so unnatural.

SECOND LORD

    My lord, I fear me it will prove too true.

KING EDWARD III

    Mother, you are suspected for his death,
    And therefore we commit you to the Tower
    Till further trial may be made thereof;   80
    If you be guilty, though I be your son,
    Think not to find me slack or pitiful.

ISABELLA

    Nay, to my death, for too long have I lived

---

75   report rumour.
       raised i.e. fabricated against.
77   sp SECOND LORD (*Lords.* Q; also at 11. 89 and 91).
80   *trial* investigation.

Whenas my son thinks to abridge my days.

KING EDWARD III

Away with her. Her words enforce these tears, 85
And I shall pity her if she speak again.

ISABELLA

Shall I not mourn for my belovèd lord,
And with the rest accompany him to his grave?

SECOND LORD

Thus, madam, 'tis the King's will you shall hence.

ISABELLA

He hath forgotten me; stay, I am his mother. 90

SECOND LORD

That boots not; therefore, gentle madam, go.

ISABELLA

Then come, sweet death, and rid me of this grief.

[*Exit* ISABELLA, *guarded*]

[*Enter* FIRST LORD *with the head of* MORTIMER JUNIOR]

FIRST LORD

My lord, here is the head of Mortimer.

KING EDWARD III

Go fetch my father's hearse, where it shall lie,
And bring my funeral robes.

[*Exit attendants*]

Accursèd head! 95
Could I have ruled thee then, as I do now,
Thou hadst not hatched this monstrous treachery.

[*Enter attendants with the hearse
of King* EDWARD II *and funeral robes*]

Here comes the hearse; help me to mourn, my lords.
Sweet father, here unto thy murdered ghost
I offer up this wicked traitor's head. 100
And let these tears, distilling from mine eyes,
Be witness of my grief and innocency.

[*Exeunt, with a funeral march*]

84   *abridge* shorten, cut short.
85   *enforce* produce, cause.
91   *boots* avails, matters.
101   *distilling* falling from (in small droplets).
102   Colophon omitted ed. (FINIS. / [Device] / Imprinted at London for *William* /
      Ihones, *and are to be solde at his* / shop, neere vnto Houlburne / *Conduit. 1594.* Q).